Encountering Other Faiths

Encountering Other Faiths

MARIA HORNUNG

Paulist Press
New York/Mahwah, NJ

Book design by Celine Allen

Library of Congress Cataloging-in-Publication Data

Hornung, Maria, 1936–
   Encountering other faiths / Maria Hornung.
      p. cm.
   Includes bibliographical references.
   ISBN 978-0-8091-4491-4 (alk. paper)
  1. Religions—Relations. 2. Communication—Religious aspects. I. Title.
  BL410.H67 2007
  261.2—dc22

                                  2007028053

Published by Paulist Press
997 Macarthur Boulevard
Mahwah, New Jersey 07430

www.paulistpress.com

Printed and bound in the
United States of America

Contents

Acknowledgments ix

Introduction xiii

1. Interreligious Dialogue in Global and American Society 1

    Need for Interreligious Dialogue in the Twenty-first
      Century 1

    The United States and the Relevance and Imperative of
      Interreligious Dialogue 10

    Imperative of Grassroots Commitment and Involvement 16

    Outcomes of Grassroots Involvement in Interreligious
      Dialogue 21

2. Interreligious Dialogue 23

    The Meaning of Interreligious Dialogue 23

    Ground Rules of Interreligious Dialogue 24

    Modalities of Interreligious Dialogue 26

    Introduction to Common Ground 30

    Major Themes of Exploration 33

    Deep-Dialogue 36

3. **Identifying a Process for Initiating
   Interreligious Dialogue at the Grassroots**...................................39

   Addressing a Lack in Adult Education Literature
       Regarding the Process of Engaging
       Religious Difference   40

   Grounding of the Process of Engaging in Interreligious
       Dialogue   42

4. **Theoretical Underpinnings to a Creative Exposure
   to Interreligious Dialogue** 45

   Milton Bennett's Stages of Intercultural Sensitivity   45

   Relating Bennett's Schema to the Process of Introduction
       to Interreligious Dialogue   52

   Fowler's Stages of Faith and Interreligious Dialogue   54

   Stages of Interreligious Dialogue   59

   Interrelating Three Models of Transformation   64

   Educational Insight into Adult Pedagogy and Personal
       Transformation   66

5. **Planning for an Introduction to Encountering Other Faiths** ...70

   Aims of This Process   70

   Basic Assumptions   72

   Basic Principles   73

   Applications   76

6. Encountering Other Faiths 78

SESSION ONE:
Gathering in Faith   80

SESSION TWO:
Assessing Our Encounters
with People of Other Faiths   83

SESSION THREE:
Exploring Religious Diversity within Our Locale   85

SESSION FOUR:
Treasuring Our Faith Heritage   87

SESSION FIVE:
Engaging in Dialogue
with People of Another Faith   89

SESSION SIX:
Exploring Common Ground
with People of Other Faiths   91

SESSION SEVEN:
Learning from Our Experiences
of Deepening Faith   93

SESSION EIGHT:
Responding to Our "Call"
to Interreligious Dialogue   96

SESSION NINE:
Envisioning a New World Reality—
Deepening Kinship,
Collaborating for the Common Good   99

Concluding Thoughts   101

7. A New Beginning..102

Notes 105

Bibliography..109

Acknowledgments

I acknowledge the many people of different faiths and ethnicities in countries throughout the world who have taught me the meaning of interreligious engagement out of an open and active pursuit of a better world reality. I acknowledge my community of Medical Mission Sisters without whom this personal engagement in the wider world might never have been mine.

I am grateful for the inspiration and encouragement that Monika Hellwig, Miriam Therese Winter, MMS, and James Redington, SJ, gave me as I undertook this journey. I acknowledge my professors at Temple University and Hartford Seminary who have enlightened and encouraged me in gaining a grounding in the foundations of major faith traditions, in interreligious dialogue, and in the practice of reflection and ministry in the pluralistic settings of our times.

I especially want to acknowledge the assistance of Helen Marr Mitchell, MMS, in the constructive work behind the editing of this book.

This book is dedicated

to all people of this world who reach out to others
in compassion and in trust

aware that while we are distinct from one another,
we do have common ground
and that together we must find that common ground.

Introduction

This book is part of a dream I have had to develop a process that introduces individuals and groups to the exciting and necessary enterprise of interreligious dialogue in its several modalities. Writing this book has been grounded in a lifetime of embracing the truth, beauty, and goodness of various religious traditions in light of being neighbor and friend, of pursuing common cause, of sharing spiritual rituals and aesthetic cultural expressions, and of finding common ground in the midst of varied dogmas and belief systems.

This book looks at the imperative of interreligious dialogue within the world and within the United States in the twenty-first century. It aims to address one of the major difficulties experienced by interested and committed people in undertaking interreligious dialogue. The difficulty has to do with where to begin and how to begin. The book creates and proposes a process model that supports interested people in becoming acquainted with interreligious dialogue.

In the latter part of the twentieth century creative work has been accomplished in the fields of cultural sensitivity, faith-development, and interreligious dialogue. Development models from each of these disciplines have been adopted to inform the basis of the process. Basic assumptions and principles for this process are elucidated. The process developed here includes: exploring religious diversity in the participants' area of interest and concern; affirming participants in their own faith articulation; engaging persons of other faiths and integrating the experience of this engagement; discerning participation in various modalities of interreligious dialogue; garnering resources and skills; envisioning global ethics dialogue; and affirming commitment to future interreligious dialogue.

The process is concretized in the nine study sessions presented in chapter 6. These sessions are not "theoretical." They are the work of heads, hearts, and hands. They guide a journey toward a deeper sense of the sacred, of the human family. The process is a way to share with individuals and groups the exciting and necessary enterprise of interreligious dialogue in its several modalities. It is grounded in a lifetime of appreciating the truth, beauty and goodness of various religious traditions as they are lived on five continents of the world.

Since the 1950s interfaith dialogue has seen momentous changes. Indeed, the spirit blows where it wills and gives birth to new possibilities. At the same time, the first decade of the twenty-first century has already seen many challenges to the concrete vision of constructive interfaith interaction. In this book I hope to offer a creative and open forum for engagement.

1

Interreligious Dialogue
in Global and American Society

Need for Interreligious Dialogue in the Tweny-first Century

Religious Traditions and the World Today

One of the great challenges facing Earth's many religions is how to preserve and even cherish unique religions and cultures and at the same time reverse the tendency for differences among them to become sources of intolerance, discrimination, division, and conflict. Democracy, which is hailed today as the panacea leading to development and peace, had its birth in the age of Enlightenment. One of the conundrums in democracies, which are an outgrowth of the benefits of Enlightenment, is that because emphasis has been placed on the individual as the foundation of the nation (state), there is no effective paradigm enabling religious and perhaps cultural entities to maintain a participative and respected status as identifiable groups within the whole. So long as an individual participates and demands rights as an individual, the system is able to grant rights and confer status (although it does not always do so). To the extent that an individual desires to participate in society as a member of a minority group within the fabric of society, he or she can be marginalized, making it necessary to fight for rights and benefits. Society is challenged to develop new participative paradigms that are inclusive not just of individuals but also of groups, whether ethnic, religious, or special interest.

Current readings, conversations, and presentations reveal that in today's world there is a rather widespread lack of understanding of religious traditions other than one's own. There is also fear, as well as hatred and violence generated by religious oppression, isolationism, or insularism and fundamentalism. Alongside all this there is strong evidence of a much smaller arena of significant and strategically important work among religious people toward deeper understanding, dialogue, respect, shared prayer, and collaboration for the general welfare. In the arena of interfaith relations, missionaries, mystics, and theologians have been in the forefront of those with high motivation and creative spirits for working toward the evolution of a new, more inclusive world reality.

People across the globe, in villages and small towns in India and Indonesia, Uganda and the United States, are more conscious than ever of being part of a larger world. Only fifty years ago most people could not have imagined the electronic communications that exploded across the world and created an awareness of being globally interconnected. Beyond connectedness, global interdependence has meant progress for some and sustained impoverishment for many. New and technologically sophisticated forms of communication also threaten a homogenization of culture and sometimes provide a vehicle for widespread expressions of interreligious animosity. At the same time, the new technology has made possible creative collaborative initiatives for justice across boundaries of nations, cultures, and religions. Some of these have engendered undreamt of success.

At the beginning of this new millennium, the potential for religion to motivate valued-based leadership is becoming more widely acknowledged. All religious traditions have people with excellent insights and creative responses to the social conditions and key issues of our times. It is also the case that within the last forty years some adherents of most world religions have engendered major movements that militate against justice, inclusivity, and peace.

In this chapter I have chosen to highlight a few of these realities. You, the reader, may prefer other realities, judging them to be more significant. In either case, we have together become more aware of the milieu in which our conversation is embedded.

Response of World Theologians, Religious Pluralists

Considerable literature covering the achievements of interreligious dialogue has been produced by theologians and religious thinkers at the global level. These writers have spoken to inclusivist and pluralist positions, mainly out of their own worldviews. They are few but very prolific, pushing the envelope of doctrinal traditions in their own religious traditions. They have achieved some wonderful results in the search for common ground among religious and ideological traditions. In this book, I have chosen to present a consensus developed by theologians and religious thinkers from many traditions.

In September 2003, a four-day summit meeting of religious pluralists, billed as the first of its kind, was held in Birmingham, England. Religious pluralists believe that all the great world religions are valid paths to salvation. (*Pluralism* is contrasted with two other predominant religious views: *exclusivism*, the belief that only within one religious tradition is salvation possible and others are excluded, and *inclusivism*, the belief that although other religious traditions contain salvific truth, only one tradition contains *all* salvific truth.) Some forty scholars (Buddhists, Catholics, Hindus, Jews, Muslims, Protestants, and Sikhs) from sixteen countries participated in the summit meeting.

I find the contribution of these theologians significant because I believe theirs is a prophetic message spoken to the global community of the twenty-first century. The summit participants articulated two versions of their text, with the second one being presented as the consensus of the summit meeting. The points of this consensus are quoted below, interspersed with some comments relating to the change in text between the first and second writing.

1. Interreligious dialogue and engagement should be the way for religions to relate to one another. A paramount need is for religions to heal antagonisms among themselves.[1]

In essence, the revised text of principle number 1 covers the same points as numbers 9 and 10 in the original. The strength of this revision is in its recognition that interreligious dialogue depends on mutual enlightenment as integral to both the motivations for and the outcomes of the dialogic conversation.

2. The dialogue should engage the pressing problems of the world today, including war, violence, poverty, environmental devastation, gender injustice, and the violation of human rights.[2]

Here the content of the exchanges between religions is delineated. It is an example of the kind of focus Aloysius Pieris, SJ, theologian and major contributor to interreligious thought and Asian liberation theology, would like to see in the encounters of people of different religious traditions. Its strength is in the compelling nature of this particular challenge to world religions as well as in the naming of this activity as a distinct arena for interreligious engagement.

3. Absolute truth claims can easily be exploited to incite religious hatred and violence.[3]

There is a significant difference between this principle and principle number 7 of the original. Here it is the exploitation of the claim to absolute truth that is the cause of hatred. The original version more clearly stated that it is actually the assertion of exclusive possession of absolute truth that causes hatred, repels people, and leads to frustration and violence. Version two says nothing about religious traditions' claim to absolute truth but simply cautions against using it to exploit others. There is no mention of the fact that the claim itself is the exploitation.

4. The religions of the world affirm ultimate reality/truth, which is conceptualized in different ways.

5. While ultimate reality/truth is beyond the scope of complete human understanding, it has found expression in diverse ways in the world's religions.

6. The great world religions with their diverse teachings and practices constitute authentic paths to the supreme good.[4]

Numbers 4, 5, and 6 make, I find, the same points as in the original. The slightly shorter versions in the revision are more direct and thus more compelling.

7. The world's religions share many essential values, such as love, compassion, equality, honesty, and the ideal of treating others as one wishes to be treated oneself.[5]

This statement of common ground among world religions is welcome as an open door to interreligious dialogue; however, I regret the loss of two concepts contained in the first version. Given the conditions in today's world, the omission of "justice" in the second version is a great mistake. Another important mistake, I believe, is the complete omission of number 5 in the first version, which points out that within the world's major religions there are forms of religious belief and practice that are used in ways contrary to those religions' own espoused values, such as compassion, equity, and a parallel of the "golden rule." To omit this is, in my opinion, to take away a grounding in humility that opens the way to interreligious dialogue.

8. All persons have freedom of conscience and the right to choose their own faith.

9. While mutual witnessing promotes mutual respect, proselytizing devalues the faith of the other.[6]

Given the task and the context of this summit, one is grateful that theologians of this caliber rose to the occasion and witnessed publicly to the world and to the leadership of their own religious traditions (sometimes a more risky endeavor) their convictions concerning the evolution of religious interrelationships.

Response of World Religions for Peace

If we were to ask people in the beginning of the twenty-first century, "What is your most urgent concern for the people of this earth?" I am convinced the answer would be, "Confronting violence and achieving a shared security across the globe." In August 2006, World Religions for Peace, the largest coalition of the world's religious communities, held its eighth world assembly. In attendance were more than eight hundred leaders of the world's major religious traditions: Buddhist, Christian, Hindu, Jain, Jewish, Muslim, Sikh, Shinto, Zoroastrian, and Indigenous religions. These leaders came to Kyoto from more than one hundred countries. The declaration issued by this assembly is worth reading in its entirety.

Before coming to an agreement on this declaration, the delegates worked in various sub-groups and networks, both structured and informal. Participants included leaders of different faith communities in countries experiencing intense conflict, such as Shi'ite, Sunni and Kurdish religious leaders from Iraq. They included leaders from different countries concerned with the same issue, such as HIV/AIDS. Their Declaration on Confronting Violence and Advancing Shared Security contains one of today's best perspectives on violence and its causes. I quote from their statement:

> Today, genocide, state-sponsored repression, terrorism, and other forms of human rights abuse violate international law, target innocent civilians, and threaten the safety of many communities. Conflict-related disease, famine, displacement and environmental catastrophes constitute serious threats to life.

> Economic injustices leading to extreme poverty and hunger kill 50,000 people each day. Preventable and treatable diseases kill millions.

> Many corporations, especially at the multinational level, set their business interests without concern for values that foster sustainable development.

> Unfortunately, religion plays a significant role in some of the most intractable and violent conflicts around the world.

> Religious communities are called not only to reject war and foreign occupation, sectarian violence, weapons proliferation, and human rights abuse, but also to identify and confront the root causes of injustice, economic inequalities, governance failures, development obstacles, social exclusions, and environmental abuses. The moral and ethical

convictions of our diverse religious traditions provide a moral foundation for confronting violence in its many forms and for suggesting a vision of shared security.[7]

The world assembly addressed its own participants as well as religious communities and governmental, international, and business sectors, urging them to develop strategies for further implementation. Included in the message to religious communities was the call to:

- resist and confront any misuse of religion for violent purposes;
- become effective educators, advocates and actors for conflict transformation, fostering justice, peacebuilding and sustainable development;
- draw upon their individual spiritual traditions to educate their members on our shared responsibilities to advance shared security; and
- network locally, nationally, regionally and globally to foster multi-religious cooperation among the world's religious bodies.[8]

In the beginning of the twenty-first century, religious communities are recognized worldwide as undeniable partners in addressing the issues of the global village. What forms will this partnership take? What answer will we make to the people of the world?

Icons of Interreligious Engagement

Journalist John Allen of the *National Catholic Reporter* has spoken of the great bondedness people all over the world felt with the late servant of God, Pope John Paul II, even when they did not agree with his traditionalist approach to certain aspects of dogma. At his death, CNN's anchors spoke of the awe-inspiring advances he had fostered in the relations between Catholics and members of other faiths throughout the world. The first pope to enter a synagogue and a mosque, he asked forgiveness for the sins of Christians, Catholics, against those of other faiths throughout the world. My hope is that, with his passing, his legacy of interreligious relations will generate new strength to enter uncharted sacred spaces.

Pope John Paul II's legacy finds company with that of Martin Luther King, Jr., Mahatma Gandhi, Yamada Koun Roshi of Japan, Blessed John XXIII, Abraham Heschel, and Anna Dengel, and resonates with the spirit of people like Abdul Sattar Edhi of Pakistan, the Dali Lama, Desmond Tutu, Jacques Dupuis, and many unnamed others. As was clearly apparent at the time of his funeral, John Paul's life-work offers us an icon of interreligious engagement for our times. This icon gives us a window into the answer to the question: *Can we become a global community, a global people, united with the sacred, with one another?* John Paul created space where many of the world's political and religious leaders sought and found a place of solace, a place to speak their own word, a place where they were listened to. They encountered a man of God, a man of integrity and compassion.

It was no coincidence that in planning John Paul II's funeral liturgy, the Vatican chose the following text for liturgical reading: "I truly understand that God shows no partiality, but in every nation anyone who fears God and does what is right is acceptable to God" (Acts 10:34–35). Mourners participating in the pope's funeral reflected an impressive religious diversity united in prayer and witness to reality here and now and to future possibility. At the papal level, John Paul pioneered in interreligious dialogue in four modalities. With the rabbi of Rome he was neighbor and friend. In advocating causes concerning international justice and peace he joined with other world religious leaders of like mind. In entering Jewish and Islamic places of worship, and in moments of common prayer, he was an ecumenical leader. And in the area of doctrinal exploration, he was forthcoming and clear. He positively encouraged the work of theologians involved in interreligious dialogue.

Truly John Paul II has been a prophetic voice in terms of engaging leaders of other faith traditions and of encouraging others to do so. At the same time, John Paul's reaction to the post–Vatican II work of some brilliant Catholic theologians resulted in the censuring of their writings. This, has, in my opinion, led to discouragement on the part of those theologians who see that, as evidenced in Vatican II documents, our understanding of dogma evolves over time. It has also resulted in some loss of credibility in terms of the Catholic Church's commitment to provide the critical thinking that can underpin a viable commitment to the reign of God among today's poor, oppressed, voiceless, and marginalized.

The United States and the Relevance and Imperative of Interreligious Dialogue

Religious Traditions and the United States Today

"The United States is becoming increasingly diverse. Perhaps the greatest challenge in U.S. society today is dealing with diversity issues—gender; sexual orientation; physically and mentally challenged people; intercultural, interreligious, and intergenerational relationships ... In the past, all who came to these shores were expected to assimilate—that is to adopt the dominant culture and language and become part of the melting pot. Today people of different origins are proud of their primary culture and try to maintain it."[9] Therefore it becomes critical to the future of this country that its citizens encounter and come to know people of different backgrounds, become familiar with their worldviews and their hopes and struggles, and enter into mutual relationships with them, as neighbors, as seekers of a just society for all, as brothers and sisters in a mutually built society.

> One clear factor of life in the United States is religious pluralism. Some may still ask the quaint question: Is the United States a Christian nation? But, put this way, it is not a question about statistical facts but an ideological slogan in response to recent events. We were pluralistic in a religious way in the 1960s, but now religious pluralism is not just an important factor, but also an essential element in our analysis. Today, there is no question that one of our features, if not our greatest strength as a nation is our religious pluralism.[10]

In the United States the demographics concerning the changing patterns of ethnicity and religious adherence give the backdrop to the country's changing value expressions and overall cultural environment. Integrating and working creatively with these toward a stronger nation requires civic participation and dynamic leadership. Making ends meet and providing for their families under current circumstances heavily impacts the priorities that demand the time and energies of most Americans. This is a significant factor in the lack of ability of many citizens to prioritize time to make their voices heard in public religious and educational arenas and to accept local-level leadership.

Hartford Seminary has published a study entitled *Meet Your Neighbors—Interfaith Facts*, which compares beliefs, practices, and vitality across Jewish, Christian, and Muslim congregations in America. These include: Mainline Protestant churches, Roman Catholic congregations, African American churches, Reform and Conservative temples, Orthodox Christian churches, Evangelical Protestant groups, and Muslim mosques. Two dimensions of this study are of interest here.

The study highlights the percent of faith community involvement in social outreach. In reviewing the statistics and graphs in this study, one sees that social outreach is a vital element of most faith communities. It is in large urban communities where most opportunities for social outreach exist. Here Christians, Jews, and Muslims are heavily engaged in meeting needs and working for a better systemic approach to issues of those made poor. It is mainly Christian groups that are present to social outreach in rural areas.

The Hartford Seminary study is simultaneously revelatory of the great lack of interfaith relations among Christian communities. In fact, for many communities of major faith traditions, this is not an operative priority. Members of African American church communities often changed the question in the survey regarding interfaith activities to one that would elicit information on interracial activities instead.

All of this is important as American society becomes more diverse. With changes in relationships and the constant evolution of values and meanings in our society, Americans face the ongoing challenge of articulating their identity as a people. This is a creative and critical challenge. If it is not attended to, Americans will less and less be able to benefit from the transformative experiences we encounter in the twenty-first century.

Convictions of Religiously Committed People in the United States

In conversations among scholars, committed religious people, and the ordinary people in mosques, temples, synagogues, and churches, the belief has repeatedly resurfaced that for religions in the United States, the most religiously diverse country in the world, this is indeed a *kairos* moment. Unlike many other *kairos* moments when it might have been assumed that if the chance to engage were not taken another moment would come, today I suspect we might not have another chance if we do not meet this challenge. It is a great one in that it asks that we all cross over into other worlds of thinking and association, at a fair distance from our comfort zones. At the same time, among religious men and women in the United States, consciousness of ecumenism, and more especially pluralism, is *not* high. This is even more significant in light of ever growing misunderstandings and conflict among religions within the United States.

In addition, interreligious dialogue is often misunderstood as something that takes place as an exchange only among experts. There is little appreciation of the various modalities of interreligious engagement, or of its benefits, benefits that outweigh the cost of beginning the engagement. There is no question that this is one of the most critically needed human endeavors in American society today. Those who have entered interreligious relationships in local, civic, and national arenas are among the prophets and healers of our times. Theirs is one of the most important contributions being made at the beginning of the twenty-first century.

The Annual Scholars' Conference (which in 2005 included Jews, Muslims, and Christians) offered insightful analyses of forces impacting interreligious engagement.[11] Some of the new threats to interreligious engagement today are September 11th and the aftermath of that attack, the provocative United States stance in a world where so many lack the means to meet basic needs and to attain self-determination, the conflicts in the Middle East and Afghanistan and Iraq, plus widespread identification of the new enemy as Muslim. Anti-Islamic sentiment is notable among many Americans and the application of new United States security measures is selectively discouraging to people of Middle Eastern origin. Both threats to and inspiration for interreligious engagement have their underpinnings in the gifts and shadows from within the religious traditions themselves.

Islamic speakers at the Scholars' Conference acknowledged that there are many things they share with Jews and Christians. Muslims too abhor the Shoah. They abhor the September 11th attacks in the United States by Islamic extremists.[12] The huge majority of Muslims simply want to lead decent lives and have their human rights protected. Yet, since 9/11, they have experienced not only insults heaped upon them, but also the deaths of great numbers of Afghans and Iraqis.

The scholars pointed out that within the Islamic tradition the Hadith has, in the minds of some, superseded the Qur'an. While the Hadith is based in an oral tradition, the Qur'an is a canonical scripture developed from the dictation of Muhammad and is held as God's revelation to humans. The Qur'an militated against oral tradition in the belief that oral traditions are not protected by God. The Hadith took on ascendancy at the zenith of Islamic power and over the centuries some people have come to view it as revelation. It is their interpretation of some writings of the Hadith that militants use to create a rationale for militancy against Jews and Christians.

Jewish scholars are aware that anti-Semitism is rampant in cyberspace as evidenced when one clicks onto websites of certain search engines. There are many other insidious ways in which anti-Semitism is promoted. Jews are passionate that the Shoah not be forgotten lest we continue to avert our gaze as modern-day genocide continues to repeat itself, and lest the world forget the milieu of anti-Semitism in which Zionism and the State of Israel were born. At the same time, while what happened to the Jewish people is truly unique and a horror in human history, the oppression and power being used against the Palestinians today cannot be condoned.

Some Jewish thinkers are of the opinion that the increasing multiethnicity of Judaism itself is a healthy challenge to Jewish self-identity. Full integration of the broad spectrum of ethnicities and nationalities in the Jewish community worldwide and the consequent shaping of the Jewish reality is not held as a concrete vision by many in Judaism. Should this vision become more widely accepted, the result could be a greater bonding of mutual concern between Jewish people and non-Jewish people of a wider range of ethnic and cultural groups.[13] It is also the case that within Judaism exclusionary texts are cited without contextualizing them in the wider Judaic non-exclusionary texts in which they are embedded.

An indisputable insight that has gained crucially needed recognition in the last fifty years is that within each religious tradition there are differences of interpretation. We live in a world that is becoming "smaller" and is marked by territorial disputes and conflicts of economic interests. We also face the politicization of religious fundamentalism in all the world's major religions. We need to be honest and open with respect to the sins all of us have committed against others. In some fundamentalist arenas, moderates of the same religion are denigrated or expelled, resulting at times in intrareligious warfare. American religious experience is one of moderation, in which lies its strength. However, insulation and isolation are also evidenced in some religious traditions in America. Can the passion of the moderates surface? How can the moderates foster a credible reinterpretation of scriptural texts?

World religions are doubtless dominant forces in society across national and economic boundaries. Religious aspirations engender local and global networks for justice and peace. Religious feelings are being used to incite and to justify war. Teachings of all the major religions do speak of the golden rule, or some variation on it, and of extending to others the same respect one wants for oneself. However, there is a need to elucidate and interpret the dogmas of these world religions in a way that leads to peace. Beyond—and flowing from—such elucidation and interpretation of dogma, interreligious dialogue must work for the elimination of ignorance, misunderstanding, prejudice, and devastation. It must seek to overcome the insecurity that leads to phobias and offer resistance to religions participating in violence. It must embrace as its goals:

(1) to move individuals and people from unawareness to understanding, (2) to move them from exclusion to reciprocity, and (3) to move them from fighting to cooperation.

However, the most critical question to arise in the beginning of the twenty-first century with respect to interreligious relationships is: How can we move interreligious engagement from the intellectual upper echelons to the classroom, to the public, to the grassroots?

Imperative of Grassroots Commitment and Involvement

In one U.S. study of religiously committed people, interreligious dialogue looms large as one of six major challenges.[14] It is an area in which few people are involved. At the same time, the areas in which religiously committed people are involved, such as service to those who are marginalized, the works of health care and education, advocacy for systemic change, witness to the rights of all, action to safeguard the environment and build communities, will require collaboration on the part of people of various religious and ideological traditions. Interreligious as well as interethnic dialogue are integral to reducing the climate of conflict in the United States and essential for preserving a nation of equality, justice, and peace.

After September 11, 2001, the professors of Hartford Seminary, themselves of different ethnic and religious backgrounds, offered their reflections in a book entitled, *11 September: Religious Perspectives on the Causes and Consequences*, edited by Ian Markham and Ibrahim M. Abu-Rabi´. The chapter that most interested me was the one written by Miriam Therese Winter entitled, "Witnessing to the Spirit: Reflections on an Emerging American Spirituality." Winter's reflections apply to people of various faiths within America. If we can admit of an emergent spirituality, then we may have provided ourselves with a sizable common ground.

Exploring interreligious dialogue in light of deepening and stretching common ground has great potential for strengthening American identity and providing good leadership both here at home and in our interdependent place with other nations in this world of the twenty-first century.

In her chapter, Winter offers some criteria for spirituality: spontaneity and openness and freedom to follow the Spirit; a capacity for the inclusion of people of many backgrounds and a view of diversity as a manifestation of the transcendent; the provision of a way of being in relationship with the sacred and with each other; the ability to transcend the divisiveness of theological differences; the provision of symbols; and, despite our shadows, the potential to always provide us with public places to witness together that we are a "nation under God, indivisible." Our spirituality holds us together as an American people and supports us in becoming who we want to be. Winter's contention is that spirituality, as an acknowledgment of the transcendent and our response to it, is not the result of September 11th but is the underpinning of that response. Thus the American response in the days and weeks after September 11th is an icon of a more perduring reality, that of American spirituality.

In an incomprehensible manner and an unimaginable way, Americans as a nation met God in the events of September 11th. What we did in that moment came from the depths of what has been, and is part of our evolving spirituality as an American people. We responded together. People of all walks of life, from different religious traditions, wept, prayed, and worked together. What surfaced to hold us together through our unspoken words, our deeds of self-offering, love, and courage, what gave meaning to the words we spoke in common prayer, in compassion for those deeply affected, in grief and perplexity, was the spirituality of a nation in solidarity.

Winter offers eight characteristics of the spirituality of American people. When these characteristics actually do underpin a group's experience, they can unite, they can offer challenge for growth, they can reveal our identity to the stranger, and they can provide expectations for the newcomer to our shores and an avenue for expressions of their gifts in a new environment. The eight characteristics are:

1. *Spontaneity*—Our reaction to September 11th was a paramount example of our spontaneity: heart-struck by the situation, sincere in responding, taking risks, and pioneering across psychic, social, and scientific boundaries. The downside of our spontaneity is our propensity for instant gratification, our lack of patience, and our limited perception.

2. *Generosity*—This is a hallmark of the American response at home and globally, offering personnel, resources, and ideas beyond the level of our comfort. On the other hand, we also have a tendency to hoard resources and ignore the devastation caused by our disproportionate use and control of world resources.

3. *Hospitality*—From its beginnings, this nation was characterized by a spirit of hospitality, of welcome founded on open doors and open hearts. This is still a hallmark of the American spirit, but it is challenged by our prejudice and racism and fear of the "other."

4. *Compassion*—Americans are capable of feeling for others in their suffering, meeting them there, and working to remove the causes. But the question before us today is: Whose suffering here at home and in other nations is able to claim this compassion and its support?

5. *Courage*—It was this characteristic that built America as a people, made homes in difficult circumstances, engendered trust, created a new form of governance, and forged a future against great odds.

Courage is needed to expand our horizons, ensure liberty for *all*, and shape our spirituality anew in changing times.

6. *Sense of community*—Across this nation, people accept others as neighbors, respecting them and working, celebrating, and deliberating together to weave the fabric of our society. At the same time, our realization of community is challenged by inequity in opportunity and access to resources and the constant pushing of the boundaries of our ethnic composition.

7. *Adaptability*—Americans are a people imprinted by a kind of adaptability that comes from a worldview that something better is possible and a conviction that we will find a way. We need to embrace the challenges and find creative alternatives so that in this country all can thrive.

8. *Patriotism*—In the Bill of Rights Americans should be able to find common ground. However, for many Americans, these truths are not self-evident. Patriotism works to make the Bill of Rights apply to all. It is a commitment to hold leaders and peers accountable for the values we espouse. "In God we trust" are words we carry with us. In today's world we know God by many names. We need a promise that that trust is never in vain.

I believe we are left with two crucial questions: (1) Can we, as a diverse population with our faith underpinnings rooted in various religious and ideological traditions, own the spirituality that represents the heart of who we are and make that ownership part of a dynamic common ground moving us forward? (2) Can we also embrace what we together see as the dysfunctionalities preventing our being "all we can be," and together from our various traditions root them out? Our future as a people depends on it.

If our American spirit is worth preserving, if we can find ground, for starters, in the American spirituality, people of various religious and ideological traditions must work in collaboration. That work can become a quest for engaging interreligious dialogue as neighbors; as makers of common cause; as people who search out and celebrate the encounter with the sacred, with the deep myth of our lives; as explorers of the truth we know and seekers of the truth we have yet to know. It can become a quest to bring to birth a new national and a new world reality.

In a recent interfaith dialogue it was mentioned that the United States has many exports, some of which we are proud of and some of which we are not. One reality that we have not yet exported is our experience of sitting down at one table as people of many faiths, as friends, as searchers for the common good, as individuals experiencing solidarity in prayer, and as seekers of common ground in terms of what we believe, especially when this requires reconciling differences in what we believe—most critically when these differences block our ability to interrelate in other areas.

We have an American ethos: all are created equal; all are entitled to life, liberty and the pursuit of happiness; all are welcome to our shores, the shores of what is now one of the most multiethnic, multireligious societies in the world. As we are challenged by national poverty, racism, and prejudice revealed in public display and surveys, marginalization of minorities in spheres of governance, religion, education, and social/economic possibility, we face new frontiers of making good on moral, organizational, and financial leadership in a world that must see to the good of all people and of creation itself. Our ethos has the power to move us in the right direction, but not unless we are willing to extend our concept of "us" to include all our sisters and brothers throughout the globe.

Outcomes of Grassroots Involvement
in Interreligious Dialogue

In 2005 the international group of scholars from the Islamic, Jewish, and Christian traditions gathered for the Annual Scholars' Conference voiced some imperatives that offer a way into the future. The image of hope was that of the wolf lying down with the lamb (Isa 65:25). We have strengthened particular communities. Together, we have to do something significantly different in terms of broader and larger communities, in terms of the global world. The competing or blocking issue is self-absorption. Leaders, as in this forum, have modeled toleration leading to unity and an ability to work together. Leaders from all three faiths have stood together to form a coalition for justice and peace. These leaders and others are questioning theological assumptions when they become exclusionary. They are examining systems that lead to hatred and violence. They are endeavoring to get at the roots of these and witnessing to alternative approaches.

Experience with interreligious dialogue leads us to be confident that respect, trust, and even friendship can grow between participants in interreligious dialogue. Deep and enriching conversations are at the heart of this dialogue. The sharing that is integral to the encounter becomes an important witness to the integrity of each dialogue partner in common exploration of religious convictions. This engenders a deepening of faith commitment as well as an enriching of belief as well. Insights into the understanding of the sacred, the human, the various ways of spiritual practice and working for the realm of justice and peace are *all* integral to the experience of interreligious dialogue. These then translate well into expectations and goals for active positive engagement in interreligious dialogue.

What are we called to do to engender this dialogic enterprise? We are called to be patient enough to do what we need to do to change; to discover how various faiths can live together; to use interreligious dialogue occasions; to develop a desire to see this society become one of greater integrity and uprightness; to work for the future of all our children, no matter what their faith; to foster the American spirit by working together through difference for greater causes; to collaborate on joint projects and common ground issues; to work proactively against all hate literature; to acknowledge our own addictions in order to go forward.

Let us be willing to look into the face of the other and hear his or her story from our heart. Let us be revolutionary about dialogue. Let us take our vision into mosque, synagogue, church, and temple.

2
Interreligious Dialogue

The Meaning of Interreligious Dialogue

Interreligious dialogue is hard work! It is also good work! Investment in this work has evidenced its great potential for being a way of relating, a way that respects all reality as subject of its own evolution, a way that leads to compassion, personal fulfillment, proactive world-building, and networking for peace. Interreligious dialogue has netted many positive results: violence stopped, creativity come alive, levels of happiness increased, destructive energy turned to creative energy, as well as growth of the authentic self.

Interreligious dialogue is an interaction between equals, between brothers and sisters. Underlying the practice of interreligious dialogue is a commitment to respect the other with no agenda to convert the other. And, when we sense that we are not yet brothers and sisters, we choose to be open to become so. When we enter our encounters, we leave behind condescension as well as attitudes of both inferiority and superiority.

In interreligious dialogue, one's dialogue partner reflects one's thoughts, hopes, and expressed values back to oneself, thus revealing another dimension about oneself and offering new choices in terms of moving toward greater congruence with one's stated values. Interreligious dialogue offers the possibility of engendering within the self a greater openness to those of other religions and their cherished beliefs, now perceived as sources of truth, goodness, and beauty. Interreligious dialogue opens the participant to widening circles of dialogue partners—supporting one's growth as a world citizen. Finally, as a person and as a follower of one's chosen religious tradition, one attains a deeper inner authority in terms of authentic religious belief and practice.

Some religious thinkers believe that the focus of religious action should be toward those oppressed or unfree in any dimension. This necessarily includes the Roman Catholic Church's preferential option for the poor but does not limit the notion of poor to only the material dimension of life. Rather, it embraces the many dimensions of physical, social, psychological, moral, and spiritual poverty from which humankind suffers. Conversely, ameliorating oppression in one of these dimensions releases potential and energy to address other forms of oppression. Two of the most critical issues that demand the concerted attention of those involved in interreligious dialogue are: (1) the call to explore the understanding of ultimate reality and (2) the call to address human rights issues. In these and other areas, interreligious dialogue has introduced new questions and concerns not previously contemplated by the participants.

Ground Rules of Interreligious Dialogue

The ground rules of interreligious dialogue, also called the "Dialogue Decalogue," originally conceived by Leonard Swidler and slightly adapted here, are as follows:

- The primary purpose of dialogue is to grow in perception and understanding of reality and to act accordingly.
- Interreligious dialogue needs to include exchange among sub-groups/traditions within religious traditions as well as between religious traditions and between religions and ideologies.

- Each participant must come to the exchange with sincerity and honesty and assume that one's partners are coming with the same dispositions.
- In the dialogue one compares ideals with ideals and practices with practices, not one's own ideals with another's practices.
- Each participant must be allowed and needs to offer his or her unique self-definition. When interpreted by another participant, the one interpreted must affirm that he or she recognizes himself or herself in the interpretation.
- No participant should come to the conversation with preconceived ideas as to where the points of disagreement lie.
- Dialogue can take place only between equals. One must assess the dimensions of equality and inequality before the planned exchange and remediate the latter if this is found to exist.
- Dialogue can take place only on the basis of mutual trust.
- Good exchange is also built upon a practice of healthy self-criticism of one's own faith tradition, beginning perhaps in areas where this tradition has made its own missteps.
- Each participant must attempt to experience the partner's religion or ideology "from within."[1]

There are two ways of naming the modalities or arenas in which interreligious engagement takes place. Swidler prefers the three modalities of: (1) the practical, in which we network with others to address problems of mutual concern; (2) the spiritual, in which we attempt to experience the spiritual expression and or practice of the other; and (3) the cognitive, in which we seek truth and greater understanding of each other. In 1991 the document "Dialogue and Proclamation"[2] articulated four forms of interreligious dialogue. These basically include the three modalities noted above and add to them the form of *neighborliness*. I favor the document's embrace of four modalities because I feel that while the last may be considered natural to all people, the fact is that it is not natural in many environments where people hardly take the time to know their neighbors of other religious traditions and ethnicities. It must be noted that in many of our American school systems and in the military, neighborly dialogue has become more natural because proactive work goes into developing relationships of intercultural sensitivity and religious tolerance.

Experience teaches that highlighting/bringing to consciousness the specific forms that interreligious dialogue can take is important because it gives clear contexts for exercising interreligious relations. It empowers participants to begin in a place that is mutually acceptable to them. It is also important because, while a given modality of interreligious dialogue may not seem feasible, one becomes alerted to the possibility that another may, in fact, be more viable. Often involvement in one form of interreligious engagement opens doors to other forms.

Modalities of Interreligious Dialogue

The styles of interreligious dialogue resonate with some of the primary patterns of interrelationship among humans in societies in general. The following highlights these ways of interrelating.

- The neighborly dimension, where we are open to one another and work to become friends in places where we live, work, and socialize together, thus creating a culture of welcome and of nurture for ourselves, for our children, and the for tasks we undertake
- The practical or "making common cause" dimension, where we collaborate to help humanity, addressing the human problems and issues that are very urgent if we are to make a difference

- The depth or spiritual dimension, where we attempt to experience the partner's religion or ideology from within or join together in rituals or aesthetic celebrations of faith and life
- The cognitive dimension, where we seek understanding of the truth, beauty, and goodness in various faiths

These four modalities of interreligious dialogue or engagement are increasingly being articulated by religious leaders and educators of different faith traditions. Religions and ideologies are not only explanations of the ultimate meaning of life but also ways of living according to the explanation. It is integral to the mission of religions that they find words to articulate these ways in the ever-changing circumstances of our lives, in the changing configurations of global reality, and in the evolving consciousness of humankind. There is a growing awareness that our concern for the well being of all people needs to be broadened to include all aspects of life. In these times, care and concern for the earth is neglected at the cost of our own peril. Each person and each society must find the delicate balance whereby the past is properly appreciated, the future is responsibly cared for, and the present is lived as fully as possible. Interreligious and interideological dialogue that does not result in action will grow hypocritical and ineffective. Action that does not invest in deeper communication and greater understanding and acceptance will grow sterile and give way to apathy. Neither dialogue nor action can survive on its own.

Dialogue of Life

Perhaps the most ubiquitous arena for interreligious dialogue is that of being neighbor to one another. Americans have a well-developed ethic of neighborliness. This is seen when reflecting on

American spirituality as described by Miriam Therese Winter, but what is also clear is that increasing diversity in our population offers us a new challenge to make good on a neighborliness, one that includes persons of different faiths and ethnicities. In our schools, in our cities and town halls, in our social and religious functions it is imperative that we discover similarities in passion and convictions and attend to the differences we experience as we engage one another. Americans have a gift for friendliness. We need to continue to work to maintain a common ground of evolving American heritage in the face of increasing religious diversity. This is the dialogue of life.

Dialogue of Action

Some human problems are so urgent that they call forth social action. This applies to neighborhood, region, nation, and world. Experience in all quarters of the world has proven that joint action is most effective. At times problems have been ameliorated only when joint action has been applied. Joint action has also resulted in breaking down barriers between groups and has enhanced the motivation to act as well as fostering greater self-understanding in the various parties.

Provocative thinkers such as Mahatma Gandhi and Blessed Teresa of Calcutta have highlighted the urgency of a preferential option for the poor. In the context of our postmodern times, this preferential option needs to include the voiceless, the oppressed, and all of us who are unfree in a whole variety of ways. Commitment to building a more just society, which is the ground of dialogue in action, includes witnessing to structural and individual manifestations of injustice, developing creative alternatives, and caring for victims of societal injustice. All of this creates new spaces of common ground and greater unity among people of different religions and cultures. This is the dialogue of action.

Dialogue of Spiritual Experience

One of the greatest sources of our sense of meaning, of our recognition of the immanent and transcendent in our midst, the wellspring of inspiration to value and commitment, is the spiritual experience into which we are drawn or which we design. This is the place where the depths of our religious attitude reside. Interreligious sharing in rituals, celebrations, silences, rites of passage, or civic liturgy involves us in a deeper than usual investment of self. Here we say with our hearts and bodies that we recognize a mutual place of encounter with meaning and a mutual affirmation of values and commitment.

The aesthetic expressions of our diverse life realities are integrally linked with the more profound experience of knowledge and recognition of our shared humanity. By way of images, insights, feelings, and rituals we enter the spaces of different meanings with an openness to experience deeply rooted in common ground. Such common ground is the stuff of understanding that supports our journey into the future. This is all integral to the dialogue of spiritual experience.

Dialogue of the Exchange of Beliefs, Dogma, and Theology

Although all of the modalities of dialogue mentioned above involve challenges, it is perhaps here that the greatest challenge to interreligious and interideological dialogue lies. One of the most crucial questions to ask: How can I speak so that on the one hand I maintain my own religious and ideological integrity, and on the other I allow my dialogue partner to understand and recognize herself or himself in my language? People who are involved in this both at the academic and institutional level as well as those involved at the grassroots level sense that our times issue a major imperative to this modality of dialogue.

Gross misunderstanding and shallow stereotypes and "-isms" used for promoting economic and political agendas are all fueled when our fears and apathy deter committed persons from engaging in this modality of interreligious dialogue. Dialogue in this area has broken new ground in the human search for truth that encompasses more and more of the human experience. Dogma and belief are enfleshed in cultural frames and often embedded in religious worldviews. Unearthing beliefs from these contexts requires that one listen and lend oneself to the context as part of the process of being able to recognize the truth spoken and finding ways to re-express it in one's own context. All of this dedicated work again paves the way to increased common ground that facilitates all the other modalities of interreligious dialogue. This is the dialogue of exchange of dogma, beliefs, and theology.

Introduction to Common Ground

We live in a milieu that is more diverse and complex than ever before—a milieu that sometimes seems very chaotic and appears to be moving in a direction opposite to the kind of world we want to see. At the same time there is in this milieu an attraction of the always-inner-movement-to-wholeness and creativity.

There is a coalescing and organizing of energy around this attraction that has given focus to the concept of "common ground"—of finding common ground and creating common ground. "Common ground" is a rich term for a reality that is captivating human consciousness. Two examples of places where this dynamic is operative are: the United Nations and ecumenical and interreligious circles.

Key Elements of Common Ground

Two key elements are integral to common ground. The concept of common ground is born in a world of great differences, among persons who are aware of these differences and of their vital importance. It is born among people convinced that there is something of great and mutual significance that they must live and work for. That something of great and mutual significance is rooted in the discovery of a mutually recognized common good: the common good of society or the common good of creation as a whole. It may be a point of survival, a cherished value, a faith conviction, a vision, or a dream. It is usually a place of great motivation.

The differences among those who work toward common ground may be cultural, spiritual, political, geographical, economic, situational, or religious. In the histories behind these differences there may be, and often are, oppressions, mutual alliances, domination, inspired evolution. The divisions may also involve differences in worldviews, presuppositions, or visions of the best response to the problem faced or strategies to use.

Creating Common Ground

Even when we don't like to acknowledge it, there is usually some, even if minimal, existing common ground among people. This already existing common ground is created or being created out of something already deeply shared: the common human condition, faith in the future of our planet, a concern for peace and security, or for acquiring basic necessities, or for ensuring that our world will be a place of healing and human flourishing. Common ground is then further created by engaging our differences in light of our common concern or hope. But those differences are not all of the same nature nor do they carry the same weight. Some differences are complementary to one another; some are analogous to one another (having different shapes in different settings); and some are truly contradictory. Part of the journey to greater common ground involves discerning the nature of our differences.

Discerning the Nature of Our Differences

Which of our differences truly complement one another and further develop our shared vision, our shared charism? It is imperative that we sustain flexibility toward creativity, toward pluriformity, toward pioneering new or alternative expressions of religious values.

Which of our differences are comparable, the same value expressed in different cultural and situational settings? Humans are committed to enfleshing values in different situations and ethnic contexts.

Which of our differences are truly contradictory and how can we discern our way to consensus in concrete situations? One touchstone has been that which is life-giving, that which will best foster fullness of life for all concerned.

Practices in the Search for Common Ground

At the heart of interreligious dialogue is finding common ground for the sake of the common good. Those who search for common ground for the common good have learned that norms of the dialogue are necessary. These center on deep listening and analytical thinking. Some of the practices include:

- Entering the dialogue with the attitude of a learner
- Trusting that all others in the dialogue are also coming as learners
- Cultivating increasing consciousness of one's own presuppositions
- Willingness to articulate shortcomings in one's own view or practice
- Being aware that one has a truth to share, but does not have the whole truth

- Being aware that each truth is best and most fully understood only in its own context
- Comparing one's own ideals with the other's ideals and one's own practices with the other's practices; that is, not comparing the other's practices with one's ideals

The aim is to increase that area of common ground so that the life and mission to which the participants are committed can flourish with greater joy, energy, and sense of shared meaning.

Major Themes of Exploration

1. *Discovery of the Sacred/Divine/Formless/God/Enlightenment/Superior Power:* How and where is one able to encounter the sacred/divine/formless/God...in your religious tradition? What sorts of experiences are seen as part of this journey of encounter? Do individuals experience a call or movement to or yearning for intimacy with "God" or with the someone or some entity beyond ordinary human experience? Are individuals called to specific paths or destinies?

2. *Prophets/Sages/Ancestors/Saints:* Are such persons important in guiding individuals toward becoming who they are called to be? Do any such persons within the religious tradition offer inspiration for living life, care for the world, creating relationships of justice and peace? How is one expected to relate to these prophets/sages/ancestors or spirits?

3. *Revelation:* What is the role, if any, of revelation in your religious tradition? Are there universally accepted beliefs? If so, what is the basis for believing? What are, for you, the main beliefs in your religious tradition? Are there intermediaries for revelation and for the interpretation of revelation?

4. Meaning of Human Life: What is the "creation story"—the story of how the world and all life began—in your religious tradition? What does your tradition/religion teach through this story about the meaning of human life and about how it is to be lived? What do humans hope for? What limitations do humans face as they strive/journey to attain that for which they hope?

5. Writings, Oral Traditions, Texts, Scriptures: What place do these have in your religious tradition? What is the ongoing relationship of believers to the writings and oral traditions? How have the interpretations of the writings and oral traditions changed or matured over time?

6. Evil: Within your religious tradition, what is the origin of evil in the world? What else do you learn about evil through your religious tradition? Are there stories that explore the origins, nature, and effects of evil as well as the roles that it plays in human lives and in the world? How are you taught to recognize and respond to evil? What delivers/redeems individuals/the world from evil? How does the sacred/divine interact with evil? What is the role of human choice, human freedom?

7. Wrongdoing: What is your understanding of wrongdoing? If sin is a concept in your religious tradition, share your understanding of it. What do you believe wrongdoing or sin is in relation to God/the sacred? How do you see wrongdoing or sin in relation to yourself or others? How do you understand sin in relation to social realities? How is one forgiven/redeemed in light of sin or evil for which one is responsible?

8. Death: What is the meaning of death for you as a member of your religious tradition? What do you believe happens after death? How do you prepare for death? What are the losses connected with the deaths of members of your communities, your friends, your family members? What helps with these losses?

What rituals are associated with death in your religion, and what are their meanings?

9. *Hope:* What in your religious tradition gives and sustains hope in the face of personal loss, oppression, or rejection, and in the midst of chaos and evil in the world? To whom or what do you turn when you are overwhelmed? As a member of your religious tradition, what do you see as positive or hopeful in the world? How is the sacred/divine/formless/God/enlightenment/superior power related to movement toward a better situation for all people and all creation?

10. *Role in the World:* What is your experience of the world? What is your analysis of the state of the world in the light of your experience? What is your personal response to your experience and analysis? Do you believe that the actions of individuals matter? What does your religious tradition say about that? How do you regard the most vulnerable persons in your society and throughout the world? What does your religion say about how they should be treated? How do individuals hope to ultimately attain salvation/paradise/enlightenment/nirvana?

11. *Transformation:* From whence comes the power to become a noble person, an enlightened person, a person of mature faith? What aspects of your faith or belief support individuals in their journeys and the community on its journey in this world? What does your religious tradition promise you? What can you count on?

12. *Community and Relationships:* With whom do you share community? What religious beliefs and/or practices contribute to the forming and sustaining of community? Do you see your religious group as community? In what sense? Do you see it as separate and isolated from the world or as part of the whole? How do you perceive your religious community in relation to communities of other religions? When differences or splits occur in your community, how

does reconciliation take place? Do you see reconciliation with other beliefs or religions as desirable? Why? Or why not?

13. Structure and Leadership in the Faith/Religious Community: How is the community of believers organized? What and who "holds together the experience" of the people of your religion as community and as a faith tradition (that is, those who have common beliefs and worship traditions)? Who exercises power? What kind of power do they have? What is the role of adherents to the religious tradition? What is the significance of the role of the adherents?

Deep-Dialogue

Swidler offers ten theoretical principles that capture and express dimensions of "Deep-Dialogue."[3] These principles, which form part of a holistic pattern of being interconnected with one another, are as follows:

1. The continuum principle: The human, in respect to faith and action, moves from a polarized position to tolerance to mutual learning to mutual transformation.

2. The dialogue-on-dialogue principle: The human considers and critiques the dialogic process itself, that it may be a place of energy and power leading into a new world (local and global) reality.

3. The reality-is-dialogue principle: The human acknowledges what science has been teaching from the sub-atomic to the cosmic level, that an interactive (dialogic) principle is basic to human reality, intra- as well as inter-personal, inter-communal, and beyond.

4. The integrative principle: Dialogic principles can move toward a destructive or integrative tendency in which the integrative tendency is a balance of forces in a dynamic whole.

5. *The critical thinking principle:* Critical thinking is an underpinning of Deep-Dialogue in which one's unconscious presuppositions become conscious, one's worldview is recognized and accepted as a single worldview among many, and another's statements can be understood in their unique context, enabling them to be translated into one's own context. Such dialogue makes it possible for one to discover the true meaning of one's own and others' statements.

6. *The knowing-is-dialogic-integrative principle:* Between the knower and that which is known the knowing itself is a dialogic, mutual, basically interactive process. This is true between subject and object, between two subjects, between communities of persons, between peoples and nations on the earth, to interconnectedness with the "Source/Goal of all reality."[4]

7. *The dialogue-is-communion principle:* The primary reason we come together in dialogue is to learn from others as well as to make it possible for others to learn from us.

8. *The pluralizing-authenticating principle:* Mutually sharing points of view can lead to understanding or enlightenment concerning authentic human living appreciated/admired in the other. This appreciation/admiration engenders the desire for further sharing.

9. *The wholeness-as-inner/inter-dialogue principle:* Dialogue initiated in the cognitive, affective, or practical areas of life spills over from its place of origination into the other two areas in a spiral movement leading to ever greater healing and wholeness.

10. *Dialogue-as-ontology-of-rightness principle:* People who have entered into dialogue experience an inner sense of rightness about their relationship with others, with the world, with creation.

Taken as a whole, these principles underpin a paradigm of human growth and integration within the religious, cultural, and ideological worlds of our age. Implementation of the principles leads to a deepened sense of one's own worldview and an awakened awareness of the worldviews of others. By offering a methodology for being transformed and contributing to the transformation of others, these principles offer the foundations of a spiritual practice. "Through this awakening power of 'Deep-Dialogue,' individuals and communities are able to experience common ground between worlds and across differences, and thus achieve deeper personal integrity and community building."[5]

To encounter and embrace common ground across differences one needs to take the initiative and accept the discipline of thinking critically. One needs to thoughtfully articulate what one means and what one doesn't mean, thus engendering a continued movement toward fuller truth. Diverse world forces challenge interethnic, interreligious encounters. Without critical dialogue regarding perspectives and worldviews, these forces threaten to remove the underpinnings of human interrelationships.

"'Deep-Dialogue' is thus the heart of our rational capacity to negotiate reality, to be in touch with ever changing worlds around us."[6] We shape our realities, even world realities, which in turn shape us. Dialogic interrelation with others affects how we act as well as how we think and speak. This type of interrelation poses a challenge to humanity today in a way not possible before. The challenge is to articulate within our global community an expected way of interacting, which can be called a global ethic. This is a viable dream, but only if more and more people personally invest themselves in the school/discipline/practice of dialogue.

3

Identifying a Process for Initiating
Interreligious Dialogue at the Grassroots

As noted earlier, the greatest challenge facing the endeavor of interreligious dialogue is the engagement of grassroots participants. There is clearly a desire in the hearts of a significant number of people to find ways to engage those of other faiths or to find ways to engage them more effectively. What is missing is a support to learning something about interreligious dialogue, to developing attitudes and simple skills that would make possible engagement in interreligious dialogue in the context of neighborliness, working on common issues, being able to feel at home with common prayer, and even to discussing personal connections to beliefs and religious practices.

Without effective support systems, it is highly unlikely that interreligious dialogue will take off at the grassroots where it is so desperately needed. As the work of Nadira Charaniya and Jane West Walsh shows, there is a dearth of material relating to support of the initiation of interreligious engagement among adults at the grassroots level. I include a summary of their study here as a building block because it gives evidence of the need for the identification or development of a model of personal and communal growth in the spirituality of a deepening embrace of the four aspects of interreligious dialogue.

Addressing a Lack in Adult Education Literature Regarding the Process of Engaging Religious Difference

"Adult Learning in the Context of the Interreligious Dialogue Process: A Collaborative Research Study Involving Christians, Jews and Muslims" is the title of collaborative research done by Nadira K. Charaniya and Jane West Walsh of National-Louis University in Chicago. This research involved twenty adults in interreligious dialogue groups lasting for more than one year. The questions asked in the research were: What is the nature of the adult learning experience in this and similar settings? Does interreligious dialogue itself facilitate ongoing discovery and understanding in the participants?

In the last few decades new religious communities have been reshaping the religious milieu in the United States, a milieu until recently dominated by Jews and Christians. The researchers state, "It is our belief, framed within a pluralistic worldview, that if we can understand how to enable the transition from being strangers with our religious neighbors to not only accepting, but deeply understanding them, we will have moved forward as a society."[1] It is imperative that this process acknowledge both the common ground and the differences that may exist between religions, and that it foster an understanding of these differences while at the same time fostering empathy as a strong characteristic of interpersonal relationships. It is also critical that these become an integral part of the process of life. The researchers attempt to address what they have found as "...a lack in the adult education literature relating to the process of crossing of borders of religious difference."[2]

At present, information regarding the interreligious dialogue process and the related learning modalities is largely undocumented and can be found for the most part among women and men facilitators across the United States. The researchers hope that their study will provide a start for building a body of literature concerning adult education and the process of initiating interreligious dialogue. In the process of their research involving Christian, Jewish, and Islamic faith communities, the authors interviewed individuals and groups, observed group meetings, and collected data regarding group facilitation. Their three primary findings had to do with: "...motivations rooted in openness and significant past experiences; interreligious learning as a threefold affective, cognitive, and symbolic knowledge construction process, and social action as inspiration and outcome of interreligious dialogue."[3] The following paragraphs highlight aspects of these findings.

Life experiences that were significant in motivation could include significant connections with persons of other faiths, a family environment of openness to or supportiveness of interreligious interactions, and personal encounters in social and political forums. Personal characteristics included curiosity about matters of faith as well as an ability to handle ambiguity. A personal sense of divine inspiration, providence, or purpose in the engagement in interreligious dialogue was important in engendering the motivation to become so involved. Institutional support, such as being invited or asked to participate in interreligious dialogue by a leader of one's faith community and provision of processes and programmatic guides, was also a motivating force.

Obvious in the researchers' findings is the fact that effective interreligious dialogue is a holistic experience involving one's sensate, intuitive, logical, psychological, emotional, and spiritual self. It was the affective domain that was associated with some of the most profound learning moments. The overall experience fostered a connected type of learning involving all of the above elements. It was a discovery of deeper meaning for oneself and shared deeper meaning created in the group.

Specifically noted in the findings were the following types of outcomes with respect to social action:

- Voluntary involvement in the committees for interreligious affairs or concerns of one's own faith community

- Increased ability and commitment to voice insights regarding the facts and nuances of meaning of another religious tradition in social and political forums
- An ability to exercise reflection and critical thought before responding to media portrayal of persons or incidents having to do with other religious traditions
- Taking personal initiative in opportunities for informal or formal ongoing education regarding other religions or interreligious dialogue
- A more constructive attitude in terms of looking for solutions to problems colored by religious conflict
- The ability to envision a new world reality as well as insights into creative strategies for working toward that reality both for this and for future generations

Specifically, the adult education model that evolved in these groups included:

> ...experiences in which knowledge was socially and collaboratively constructed...a process of listening, hearing, questioning, relating, symbolizing, feeling and story telling...revising and enlarging of narratives related to religious teachings, religious beliefs...spirituality...being renegotiated as we interact with others who are of different cultural and spiritual backgrounds...incremental transformative learning...linked to the learner's cognitive, affective and symbolic domains of meaning making.[4]

Grounding of the Process of Engaging in Interreligious Dialogue

No movement into interreligious dialogue will take place or last very long unless it is grounded not only in an appreciation of the global human reality we face but also in: a worldview that embraces the Source of Life, as well as an appreciation for the validity of human response to the Source of Life through a commitment of one's own life; a respect for equality in dialogue among communities of diversity; and a valuing of proactive collaboration among people toward justice and freedom as essential to the common evolution of the whole. All of this, in turn, needs to flow from the experiences and intuitions of real live participants, journeyers together toward the creation of a new world reality for themselves and their children.

Movement into interreligious dialogue is not to be rooted in a rejection of or denigration of one's own religious tradition. It is to be rooted in an honest search for truth, beauty, and goodness in one's own and others' religious traditions, energized by the conviction that truth, beauty, and goodness are not fully manifest in any one tradition but exist in potential in all. Acceptance of the shadow sides of any religious tradition is a healthy and necessary stance as one enters the process of intentional interreligious dialogue.

In the world of today, no one set of assumptions can serve as a foundation to all theological and ideological enterprises. There is no one right way to the exclusion of the ways of all others. Given these two facts, there is great value in working things out in dialogue. It is here that the way to a better life and a better world order is found. Building up the human family requires multidimensional exchange as an essential underpinning. Indeed, the sacred is known only in part by humans; the totality of the sacred has an unknown face.

In my encounters with people of many countries, cultures, and religions I have been delighted to continue my search for God and know that I have met God in many places and under many guises. I have come to carry the whole world's concerns in my heart. Interreligious dialogue has become a passion with me. I am an integral part of an intercultural, international group of healers who have

> whole lifetimes of cultural immersion, of openness to various religions, and [seek] to exclude no one in our care

and concern. This has brought us to a new awareness that inclusiveness marks our presence in the world. We have come to understand that the primacy of love is the most enabling force that there is. This allows us to respect difference, honor diversity and open ourselves to faith we find beyond the boundaries of any religion's claim to the "one true faith."

We have found so much beauty in diversity that we relate to God as a God of inclusivity...We have discovered the value of working things out in a dialogic way. This is another way of honoring different perspectives and working through them. We have been challenged to do this work for mutual understanding with other cultures and faiths and with the church. Through trial and difficulty, grace has come with the decision to stay in the dialogue.[5]

4

Theoretical Underpinnings to a Creative Exposure to Interreligious Dialogue

Milton Bennett's Stages of Intercultural Sensitivity

The Bennett model of the pathway to greater cultural sensitivity has six basic stages. Three of these are termed "ethnocentric," stages in which one assumes that "the worldview of one's own culture is central to all reality."[1] Three are termed "ethnorelative," stages in which one assumes that "cultures are only understood relative to one another, that a particular behavior can only be understood within a cultural context."[2]

There are similarities between the concepts of ethnocentricism and egocentricism. The most obvious similarity is that the self or one's own culture is seen as central to how one, as well as others, engage the world. In the ethnocentric stages, the experience of cultural difference is threatening.

In the ethnorelative stages, the experience of cultural difference is non-threatening. This is because people in these stages, while preferring one particular culture, do not perceive cultural difference as good or bad and surely do not see their own cultural worldview as central to all others.

The three ethnocentric stages are denial, defense, and minimization; the three ethnorelative stages are acceptance, adaptation, and integration.

Denial

The first stage of ethnocentricism is denial. It is a stance in which cultural difference is not part of one's world reality, because either one is in fact isolated from people of other ethnic origins or one has insulated oneself against the consciousness that culturally different people exist, or because the society in which one lives has segregated culturally different people, thus making it possible not to encounter them at all or to encounter them only in stereotypical roles or places.

Because persons in this stage may not be actively involved in personal violence toward the other, it may be seen by them as a benign stage. The dangerous impact of this stage is that it relegates others, such as those of minority cultures or of different faith traditions, to a subhuman status. Another negative impact of denial is that segregation from others can result in people becoming more and more isolated, thus breeding more local or international tension.

Defense

The second stage of cultural sensitivity represents the attempt to counter the impact of the cultural difference that one experiences. The difference encountered is a threat to one's sense of reality and one's identity. There are basically two forms of defense.

1. *Denigration:* This is a basically negative evaluation of the other. It is often manifested in the attribution of negative characteristics to all members of an ethnic group. What can help is an awareness of the inevitability of denigration and of the importance of naming it as a progression out of denial and toward greater cultural

sensitivity. Supporting the building of self-esteem in persons of minority groups can facilitate development here.

2. *Superiority:* This is an overemphasis on the positive evaluation of one's own cultural status. We reduce the threat of cultural difference we experience by implicitly relegating it to a lower status. What can help is affirming the speaker's culture and then lifting up the equally good qualities of the other culture.

Minimization

This stage of cultural sensitivity minimizes the uniqueness of different cultural realities, stressing the nature of cultural similarities. Minimization takes two primary forms.

1. *Physical Universalism:* This is the naive "assertion that, despite differences, all people share the same basic characteristics,"[3] such as motivation for achievement. Almost always these characteristics seen as universal are those native to and prized by the speaker's own culture. What helps here is the presentation of the findings of appropriate anthropological and sociological studies that evidence the significant grounding of human behavior in the context of the society and situation from which the person comes.

2. *Transcendental Universalism:* This perspective begins by viewing all human beings as coming from the same transcendent or sacred origin. However, the supernatural force assumed to ground cultural differences is invariably derived from one's own worldview. What helps here is to find a way out of relying on one's own beliefs and assumptions as absolute and to acknowledge affirmatively the pluriformity of beliefs and assumptions that are integral to cultural entities.

Acceptance

One enters the stage of acceptance after having begun to reckon with a non-absolutist position vis-à-vis cultural goodness. In this stage one acknowledges, respects, and accepts cultural difference as an essential and preferred human condition. It is the first of what are called the "ethnorelative stages." Thus, an important paradigm shift in one's thinking and assumptions underpins this stage.

One owns the fact that one has a worldview. The most significant thing is that one sees one's worldview as exactly that, a view on the world or an organization of the phenomena of life, a vantage point from which one is able to relate—as a peer—with the worldview of the other. One recognizes one's own worldview as culturally (as well as historically, politically, and spiritually) determined, just as the worldview of the other is culturally determined. In the world of interreligious dialogue, a similar paradigm shift is required. Unless one can embrace the fact that truth can be found in other religions, that an understanding of the sacred as well as effective spiritual pathways can be found there, then one is not able to truly enter into dialogue.

There are two aspects to acceptance.

1. *Respect for Behavioral Difference:* This is acceptance of the fact that all forms of verbal and nonverbal behavior vary across cultures and the belief that all forms of behavior are worthy of respect, even if one does not personally support the behavior.

2. *Respect for Value Difference:* Attaining respect for value difference calls for another shift in our orientation to reality. We begin to see that we do not possess values and assumptions, but rather, that we assume things that allow our world to be organized in a certain way. We come to understand that we "value or assume relative goodness or rightness about phenomena which emerge from our organization of the world."[4]

In the stage of acceptance we recognize that the way other cultures value is different—and is worthy of understanding and respect. At the same time, we realize that we need not agree with the way another culture values. What helps to further intercultural sensitivity is an emphasis on the practical application of ethnorelative acceptance to intercultural communication.

Adaptation

Using the development that has been occurring on the level of acquaintance with, appreciation for, and great interest in cultural diversity, and having come to the realization that one's cultural worldview is only one of many, a person begins in this stage to acquire more skills in relating to those of other cultures. This happens *not* at the expense of denigrating one's own cultural ways, but as an adding of others' cultural practices to one's own.

Another paradigm shift is possible here. One can see that one does not have or own a culture, but that one engages a culture. One thus becomes able to select a culturally appropriate response to a situation different from the one with which one was brought up. There are two frames of reference for shifting one's cultural frame of reference and consequently one's behavioral expression.

1. Intentional Empathy: This involves comprehending or imagining another's perspective. One consciously and temporarily shifts one's worldview and participates in the other's.

2. Pluralism: Webster's definition of pluralism is: "a state of society in which members of diverse ethnic, racial, religious or social groups maintain an autonomous participation in and development of their traditional culture or special interest within the confines of a common civilization"; also "a concept advocating this state."[5] What is characteristic of this aspect of adaptation is the "internalization by one individual of two or more fairly complete cultural frames of reference. It is felt that the minimum time spent in a different culture to be able to do this at a rudimentary level is two years."[6]

Pluralism may be accidental, if it has been achieved without one's having moved through the learnings of earlier stages. This can happen when people adapt to life among those of another ethnic heritage without having been prepared for this or remain unconscious of the nature and relevance of adaptations they have made. They may be able to understand and respect differences with which they are familiar, but this sensitivity and ability may not be able to be utilized in a more general way when encountering other cultural differences with which they are not familiar. What helps development beyond adaptation is accessing opportunities for increased intercultural interaction.

Integration

The sixth and final stage of intercultural sensitivity is integration. Two key aspects of this stage are contextual evaluation and constructive marginality.

1. Contextual Evaluation: It must be noted that, in Bennett's scheme, up to this stage of ethnorelativism, difference has been seen not as good or bad, but simply as other. In this stage one attains the capacity to assess situations using cultural perspectives that have become one's own as the outcome of effective acceptance and adaptation.

One is able to frame a situation within an appropriate cultural context and has the self-awareness to exercise choice about one's response. The ability to use more than one style of response is adaptation. The ethical consideration of which style to use in a given situation is a skill of integration. Persons in this stage see their identities as including many cultural options, and they can make choices about these without losing their sense of identity. Persons can assess the strengths and weaknesses of their own culture. They do not feel the necessity to embrace their own culture in its entirety. They are able to discern the aspects of a dominant culture that sustain oppression without rejecting the entire culture.

2. *Constructive Marginality:* In the integrative stage the person has made "a commitment to a value system honed from many contexts. He or she has an identity actively based solidly on self as a choice maker."[7] He or she has the ability to empathize with others, balanced by the skill of evaluating within the cultural context. The person is able to both define boundaries and be flexible with boundaries.

Commitment within pluriformity is typical of constructive marginality. Persons in the integrative stage value all of their cultural identities; they feel authentic and never *not* at home. They are reflective, capable of action and commitment, able to take risks and to tolerate a great amount of ambiguity. Effective functioning at this stage requires psychological integration capable of engendering a commitment to justice and world consciousness.

Such persons live between worlds and are dynamic.[8] Often people in this stage have more in common with their peer constructive marginals than with people of their original culture, sometimes even members of their own families.

Constructive marginality differs from "encapsulated marginality," a phrase used to describe the situation of being trapped between or caught on the margins of different cultural realities without having chosen to be there. This can occur when people are abruptly placed in situations without having chosen or been prepared to be there. The result can be vulnerability and diffuse identity as well as anxiety and disorientation. Some of the characteristics of encapsulated marginals are "difficulty in decision-making, alienation...self-absorption,"[9] and never being at home. Among the most likely causes of encapsulated marginality are oppression and other forms of violence and injustice in a person's life. These realities need to be dealt with and some reconciliation sought.

Encapsulated marginality can be the grounding for a strong sense of cultural realities (justice issues) and can create an awareness of the need for conscious personal choice as well as insights and skills leading to constructive marginality. With attainment of the state of conscious choice and the construction of good boundaries, a person may become a constructive marginal.

Relating Bennett's Schema to the Process of Introduction to Interreligious Dialogue

How does developing interreligious sensitivity parallel the concept of developing intercultural sensitivity? Religion, which supports societal development as well as an experience of and relationship with the transcendent, is a heavily cultural phenomenon. Stages of interreligious sensitivity could easily parallel those of intercultural sensitivity: denial, defense, minimalization, acceptance, adaptation, and integration. However, the final stage (integration) may more likely be defined as fully participating in one's own faith worldview and practices along with great understanding of and collaboration with those of other religious traditions. Except where syncretism is acknowledged and understood as such, only a small percent of people will see bi-religiousness as parallel to biculturalism. Here, of course, is where the notion of a global spirituality can transcend the issues and create a new paradigm of human encounter embracing both particularity and deep universal connection.

The phenomenon of denial resulting from geographic isolation from or intentional segregation from or apathy regarding other faith traditions is alive and well. The impact of denial with respect to those of other faith traditions, often mixed with cultural denigration of others, has resulted in the relegation of people to subhuman status, unabated oppression, suspicion, hatred, and violence. For most people it is a short distance to recognizing this as a phenomenon in today's world; however, it is a *long* distance to making the organized effort to leave the comfort zone isolation has provided. Also, even if one can see the need, prioritizing time and energy to study and to interact is difficult. Using the Bennett model, one can gain insight that it is imperative to make the journey to interreligious engagement.

Significantly, Bennett posits a major shift in worldview or paradigm between the stages of ethnocentricity and ethnorelativity. It involves the abandoning of one's innate sense that one's person, with one's own cultural perspective, is the center of everyone else's worldview. To do this one must pass through and then *beyond* the stage of denying that other cultural worldviews exist and are authentic and relevant for those who hold them, and that these traditions may have something to add to one's own cultural perspective. Second, one must also grow beyond the need to use denigration of others or interaction from an erroneous position of superiority as ways of reducing the threat of difference. Third, one must embrace the vital function of difference in building up society, and begin the process of critical thinking necessary to avoid characterizing all people as the same, as being in one's own cultural mode.

Interreligious dialogue posits a paradigm shift in one's worldview, a non-absolutist stance from which one can accept that other religious traditions in their commonalities and differences—analogous, complementary, and critical—have a place in this world. This non-absolutist stance urges one not only to acknowledge the right of other religious traditions to be sustained and protected but also to consider their effectiveness as ways of encountering the transcendent and as paths to salvation and visions of how to build a better human society. A fruitful pedagogical process may well invest time at the early stages in addressing forms of denial, defense, and minimalization.

The stages of acceptance and adaptation have practical relevance in drawing program participants into logical activities that provide the kinds of experiences that lead to integration in practicing interreligious dialogue. Practice in the skills of adapting to as well enjoying and slowly feeling at home with those of other faith traditions can be very helpful. The aspect of contextualization holds the promise of supporting people in thinking critically and eventually in synthesizing new constructs for sustaining dialogue.

Fowler's Stages of Faith and Interreligious Dialogue

After years of research and reflection, James Fowler proposed an identification of what he termed were stages of faith development.[10] "We looked at faith as a way of knowing and seeing the conditions of our lives in relation to more or less conscious images of an ultimate environment... All of these play critical roles in shaping our actions and our reactions in life."[11] Fowler's stages of faith comprise the following: Intuitive-Projective faith, which an infant receives directly from the nurturing and teaching of parents or parent figures; Mythic-Literal faith, in which one absorbs literally the myths, beliefs, and practices of the community in which one is immersed; Synthetic-Conventional faith, in which one owns a world of meaning that is shaped by the larger community to which one adheres and out of whose attitudes and values one shapes one's behaviors and evaluates what is good and evil—strongly conforming to that community's conception of an ideal adult; Individuative-Reflective faith, in which one's identity is now grounded in a reflected and acquired worldview with a sense of meaning differentiated from that of others; Conjunctive faith, in which one integrates aspects of faith perspective or worldview, values, and attitudes left aside in gaining the clarity and focus of the Individuative-Reflective stage of faith; and Universalizing faith, in which persons "become incarnators and actualizers of the spirit of an inclusive and fulfilled human community."[12]

In general I have observed that most adults find their home in stage three (Synthetic-Conventional faith) of Fowler's paradigm. They have a worldview that embraces people beyond their own family, including people in their social, occupational, religious, and ethnic circles. If it includes persons of other ethnic groups, the exchange is based in limited or role-type interactions. Their faith does not inspire a lot of interest in or concern for such people. As long as competing interests can be satisfied and other crises do not loom on the horizon, interactions are generally civil and disinterested. Two of the American exceptions to this are the school system (especially in urban areas) and the military, where ethnic mixes are great. These systems are shaped to engender a worldview that can sustain respectful interaction among all parties. The traditional faith community of the individual may or may not support this development. Whether it does or not is likely to depend on whether the faith community itself is multiethnic.

What are the implications for interreligious interactions? Significant others in the communities of which one is a part play a vital role in shaping one's expectations and value articulations. An important facet of this stage of faith is that values and many principles that engender response remain tacit or under-articulated. Untested assumptions tend to be pervasive. The traditional figure of authority in the community or the "consensus" of a peer group is the usual reference point as to what is acceptable and even ethical. One looks to such authority to validate one's worldview and for a sense of whether one is worthy or valuable or esteemed. For those who adhere to a faith tradition (most Americans), this environment retains significant power after school and military service is completed.

From this stage there can emerge a personal sense of one's own story, its origin and its future, along with the challenge to interact in the present to shape this story. While remaining in this stage can yield a significant sense of comfort and reassurance, there are certain pitfalls. For example, internalization of the evaluations and worldviews of others can jeopardize the development of one's inner authority; betrayal by significant others can result in despair about ultimate being or a relationship with an intimate God unconnected with life relationships. Without a compelling personal experience that provokes questions or urges one into alternative ethical choices, many people will remain in this stage of faith. Interreligious relations at any depth are very unlikely to be engaged.

Several things can provide the backdrop for a call to transition to the next stage of faith.

- Contradiction between two or more valued sources of authority
- Significant changes in the traditional community's worldview, values, or practices
- Life events that cause one to critically reflect on the worldview, sense of meaning, values, and practices held by one's community, paving the way to see these in small or large part shaped by the dimensions of that community culture or situation and thus not necessarily universal

Leaving home literally or figuratively paves the way to critique meanings and values and to begin to own new ones, thus engendering the transition to the next stage of faith. My interactions with people have evidenced that the movement from stage three to stage four of faith can occur in select areas of one's life and does not necessarily involve the same change in all areas of life. However, such change is the thin edge of the wedge to becoming a person increasingly guided by one's own inner authority.

Most significant in the fourth stage (Individuative-Reflective faith) is that one's identity and the creation of one's own abstract faith constructs are no longer sustained by the traditional network of significant others or through adherence to roles but grounded in a reflected and acquired worldview. One's sense of meaning is differentiated from that of others, and the major contributions to one's interpretations and analyses are responses to one's own and others' actions. Demythologizing is characteristic of this stage as well as a tendency to absolutize one's now unique critical thinking with regard to the assessment of realities, symbols, and beliefs, assimilating others' perceptions into one's unique worldview.

What is the impact of stage four on the impetus for interreligious interaction? Often it is the encounter with the faith stance of an individual of another faith tradition or with someone who has herself or himself moved beyond stage three that enables one to meet the personal challenge of transition to stage four and beyond. Surely stage four of faith lays the ground for a de-absolutization of elements of one's traditional faith heritage at least in some areas of life.

Various inroads are made into what was a somewhat neatly constructed worldview and commensurate attitudes and behaviors. These are likely to come from one's inner deposit of intuition, images, feelings, affections, symbols, myths, paradoxes from within one's own tradition or that of others strong enough to claim one's attention; allegiance compels one to want to integrate them into a more balanced or holistic framework of life, "... toward a more dialectical and multileveled approach to life truth."[13]

The fifth stage (Conjunctive faith) is the one in which a person is impelled toward an engagement in the deeper reality of life. The unique and authentic concepts and values that grounded a vibrant stage four of faith are experienced as poles in a more integrated faith perspective in which still other faith perspectives are accommodated within a more integrative frame of reference. One reworks and reclaims one's past. One is more attentive to and integrative of the insights of one's inner self. One discovers and ameliorates one's general unconsciousness concerning structural injustice, especially if this injustice may have been engineered by or to the advantage of one's group of ethnic or faith origin or social class. "Alive to the paradox and the truth in apparent contradictions, this stage strives to unify opposites in mind and experience."[14] The results of this inner movement are a commitment to justice freed from the radical biases of culture, religion, political or economic entities, and the attraction to using oneself as a resource in assisting others to develop both a more individualized reflective faith and a more integrative, inclusive, and generative faith stance.

Fowler sees in this stage a "...capacity to see and be in one's or one's group's most powerful meanings, while simultaneously recognizing that they are relative, partial and inevitably distorting apprehensions of transcendent reality."[15] Stage five enables one to appreciate the truth, beauty, and goodness to be found in the symbols, rituals, and myths of one's own and other faith traditions. At this point one can opine that stage four readies a person for the phenomenon of interreligious interaction and its necessity in today's world. Proactive and creative engagement in interreligious dialogue can begin in stage four and will blossom in stage five. It is the stage-five person who has the faith and conviction to witness to the possibility and imperative of interreligious dialogue and can support others in acquiring the faith and the capacity to converse across religions in the four modalities of interreligious dialogue.

Transition beyond stage five is not a common human phenomenon. A stage-five person's inclusivity and genuine appreciation of his or her own faith and faith tradition as well as that of others is a rarity in our world. The general lack of such vision, laying the groundwork as it does for continual animosity, exclusion, misunderstanding, projection, stereotyping, self-interest, hatred, and violence places the stage-five person in a markedly liminal space. The stance in this space is characterized by having one foot in the vision of a transformed world and one foot in an untransformed world.

Stage six involves a radical actualization. Persons who out of their faith and trust lay their lives on the line for the sake of a fulfilled human community, one in touch with and caring for everything that lives, have generated a worldview in which the sacred/God/ultimate environment is "inclusive of all being."[16] They create spaces of possibility for moving toward a world freer of crippling and oppressing political, religious, social, economic, and cultural conditions—toward a new world reality. Their processes frequently call into question the familiar structures on which we base our sense of security, perhaps even our survival. These prophetic individuals are often persecuted. Fully integrated human beings with a great sense of clarity, directness, and simplicity, they love life yet hold it loosely and are open to interaction/friendship/dialogue with people at any stage of faith in any faith tradition. Theirs is a universal community of humankind, of the whole web of life.

Stages of Interreligious Dialogue

The third essential underpinning of an introduction to interreligious dialogue is interreligious dialogue itself.

Leonard Swidler has devoted over thirty years to the work of interreligious dialogue and even more years to the study of religion and theology. He has studied the major religions of the world and been involved in dialogues between most of them. In the reflections that follow, I draw on some of Swidler's concepts in the book, *The Study of Religion in an Age of Global Dialogue*, which is co-authored by Paul Mojzes. I begin with the definition of religion enunciated in the book:

> Religion is an explanation (creed) of the ultimate meaning of life and how to live (code) and structure (community) accordingly, which is based on the notion of the transcendent with which the believers have a relationship (cult). Because religion is an explanation of the ultimate meaning in life, it provides a code of behavior in the fullest possible sense, including all the psychological, social, and cultural dimensions of human life, and is hence a way of life for humans. The way of life that religion tries to provide is not, however, just a more or less acceptable way of life. It is an attempt, on the basis of its "explanation" and experience, to put forth the best possible way of life.[17]

Religions support their adherents in defining the goal of life and in determining the best way to reach that goal. The religious tradition suggests to its adherents that they will become authentic and fully human persons as a result of following this way. Within the paradigms they espouse, they offer "salvation" to their true followers. Theists and non-theists have unique worldviews. It is our experience that theists, in dialogue with non-theists, can make room for a non-personal understanding of ultimate reality; non-theists can make room for an understanding of Ultimate Reality that is personal. A fuller development of the understanding of what it means to be fully human can be enlightened by dialogue between adherents of different ideologies and religions.

One's own self-definition and the definition of one's community are intimately bound up with one's worldview or religious tradition or ideology. Thus one is vulnerable to contact with or confrontation by different worldviews and value expressions. Without the cultivation of sensitivity to and/or dialogue with others, conflicts of rather great magnitude can ensue. Thus, if humans are to avoid even more oppression and violence, they must enter into interreligious or interideological dialogue.

Over the last fifty years this dialogue has been taking place in many settings. Religious scholars and leaders of various religious traditions have been at the forefront of this effort, which has led to the discovery of new worlds of mutual understanding of life's ultimate meaning and the ways in which humans can respond together to life's challenges. The effort has gradually broadened, and people at local levels are being urged to engage in dialogue thoughtfully and critically.

> Dialogue is a conversation between two or more persons with differing views, the primary purpose of which for each participant is to learn from the other so that he or she can change and grow...both partners (sharing) their understanding with their partners. We enter into dialogue, however, primarily so we can learn, change, and grow, not so we can force change on the other.[18]

Clearly we do not want to enter into dialogue so that we can gain enough information to deal with or convert others or to debate with them. We aim to understand the other's religious or ideological worldview from his or her perspective. There will be times when we may find the other's stand or perspective so compelling that in integrity we need to integrate something of this perspective into our own, for example the inspiration of *ahimsa* or non-violence of Gandhi. It is a rather recent development in human history that we could believe that our grasp of truth, goodness, and beauty could be deepened through dialogue. This has much to do with the rising level of human consciousness as well as intellectual and reflective maturity. Inherent in human maturity is the call to take on a dialogic pattern of life.

Some of the external reasons that initiate the demand for dialogue are the exponential rise in migrations of people as well as the travel of people to other parts of the world for business and pleasure; the omnipresent mass media which inveigles its way into our perceptions, attitudes, and opinions; and the interdependent nature of global economics. Isolation is no longer a possibility. Because of the refusal to dialogue we have wars, starvation, and ecological disasters. Ignorance and prejudice can no longer be met with indifference. Dialogue and cooperation are our only alternative. Many among the world's religious traditions are more forcibly recognizing this.

Swidler and Mojzes outline what many have experienced as the seven stages of "Deep-Dialogue."[19]

Stage One—Radical Encountering of Difference: Early encounters with those of other religions are inherently challenging and even threatening as I face a new worldview, a new way of interpreting reality, and new ways of responding that are clearly other. I am tempted to appropriate the other to my own worldview. I soon realize that this disruption to my worldview and ways of responding won't go away, nor will it accommodate my own worldview and ways of responding. I may be tempted to withdraw from the situation, only to discover that my place in society may not allow for such withdrawal. The decision to proceed moves me on into the second stage.

Stage Two—Crossing Over—Letting Go and Entering the World of the Other: As I make the decision to engage the world of the other sincerely I find myself called to explore, to learn anew and to reassess my norms regarding adequate and appropriate expressions of values, and to critique my traditional attitudes. I find that I need to approach the new worldview with openness and a bracketing of my stereotypes and prejudices. As I do this, I find myself moving into stage three.

Stage Three—Inhabiting and Experiencing the World of the Other: The experience of empathy and interest then expands into a sense of freedom that opens doors to learn many things from this other world: what is of greatest importance, modalities of interaction, what causes suffering to those in this world. As I experiment with integrating ways of thinking and acting in light of my discoveries, I sense an excitement and a deepening relationship with those of this world. At a certain point, after I have gained some competence in negotiating this environment, I discover that this is not my true home. This moves me into the fourth stage.

Stage Four—Crossing Back with an Expanded Vision: The new knowledge I have gained in alternative ways of thinking and acting is now part of my repertoire as I regain my sense of belonging in my own world. I am able to think and act from both perspectives as the context may require. My own sense of identity has deepened, has changed, and no matter what choices I freely make to believe and to act, I can no longer assume that my former unilateral way of being in the world is the only way. My attitudes and concerns are irrevocably reshaped to hold the other in view, in relationship. This moves me into stage five.

Stage Five—The Dialogic Awakening—A Radical Paradigm Shift: I experience a profound shift in my worldview as well as expanded consciousness of concerns and needs and causes of dysfunction in world realities and viable ways of human response. I can no longer return to my former worldview that did not have a place for this other. Further, I am irrevocably shaped to the possibility that there is a plurality of viable worldviews, concerns, and human responses. This changes my sense of myself. I become aware of the interconnectedness of myself and many/all others, including Earth and all her needs and potentials. This awakening is what moves me into the sixth stage.

Stage Six—Global Awakening—The Paradigm Shift Matures: This stage of Deep-Dialogue opens me to the common ground that underlies the multiple worlds with which I am surrounded. I can perceive that the unique differences essential to these worlds are contained in a field of unity. My own inner world is now apparent as a range of perspectives and unique to myself. I am increasingly open to dialogue with others in my various communities of life, to a transformed relationship with them and an embrace of the context in which these communities are situated. There is for me an expanding world of communities of life with greater potential for ongoing dialogue, new learning, and deepened relationships. This moves me to stage seven.

Stage Seven—Personal and Global Transforming of Life and Behavior: One of the most significant transformations that has taken place on this journey is a greater and more encompassing moral consciousness and ensuing practice. The communion that I experience with all—self, others, and the Earth—is profound. I sense that my care for myself, instead of being in competition with concerns for the welfare of other realities, is integral to the care of the whole. As I come to deeper self-realization and greater self-fulfillment, I experience deeper meaning in relationships and in my whole life.

Interrelating Three Models of Transformation

I have annotated the developmental models: Stages of Faith, Stages of Cultural Sensitivity, and Stages of Interreligious Dialogue because together they shed light on the journey to an inclusive, interactive, collaborative engagement of people of different religious traditions. Each of these models identifies a stage in which the human person achieves a developed worldview, a set of values, a way of interrelation with others and a mode of responding to the world he or she inhabits.

Fowler's stages of faith best highlight for the reader the basic dynamics of how a person arrives at the stage described above. Fowler's stage three (Synthetic-Conventional faith) best describes the dimensions of this stage. This becomes an important foundation for the other two models, which acknowledge this stage but do not describe it sufficiently to provide a developmental process that meets the participant where he or she is.

Each of the models envisions and encourages a transformative process which, when engaged, supports individuation, a deeper sense of integrity, inclusivity of others, and an ability to speak to a global reality in a constructive way. This represents the last stage in each of the respective models. Fowler will say such a person is "inclusive of all being";[20] quoting Muneo Yoshikawa, a contributor to the Bennetts' research into ways of intercultural sensitivity, Janet Bennett says this person is engaged in "dynamic in-betweenness";[21] Swidler himself says the self lives and acts in a new dialogic consciousness.

Fowler's stages of faith are most informative with regard to the dimensions of the transformation the person undergoes. Because of this, I find that one best roots an introductory process by situating its starting point at the end of Fowler's stage three, in which personal experience or conviction has already prompted the movement into stage four. The process is designed to accompany the journeyer in his or her engagement with stage four and in the incipient desire to engage in stage five. In the end it also gives a glimpse of stage six, supporting a growing vision within the heart of the journeyer.

The stages of transformation in the interreligious dialogue process focus the content of the hoped-for transformation. The process is shaped by a desire to make a proactive commitment to interreligious dialogue in this world. The basic movements of crossing over and back, developing a vision and engaging the dialogic process, give substance to the ongoing commitment of the journeyer. These movements continue to be repeated at ever greater depth as commitment unfolds and the arena of its involvement widens in ever expanding circles.

Bennett's model best elucidates the many aspects of the psychosocial process that faces people as they move from a place of ethnocentricism to one of ethnorelativism. There is a rather direct translation of these phenomena into the journey from religious exclusivism to interreligious dialogue. It becomes essential to build in attentiveness to denial, defense, and minimization as the individual encounters, in a significant way, those of other religious traditions. It is likewise essential to encourage the journeyer through the stages of acceptance, adaptation, contextual evaluation, and constructive marginality.

Fowler's stages of faith affirm the organic nature of the evolution of faith into the end point posited by the stages of interreligious dialogue. It is important to remember that the stages of interreligious dialogue will outlast a simple introductory process. They will give the journeyer a paradigm for continuing the commitment to interreligious dialogue.

Educational Insight into Adult Pedagogy and Personal Transformation

Dorothy Ettling of the University of the Incarnate Word in San Antonio has done valuable work in the area of adult education and modalities that foster personal transformation and engender a commitment to engage in social change. In her presentation at the 2001 meeting of the Adult Education Research Conference (AERC) she discussed elements of the transformative approach, which include the significance of relationships, multiple ways of knowing, linking to core values, storytelling, and mutuality among participants. She also indicated some of the further implications of that model of education for leadership for social change.[22] Her insights can be applied to creating a model of adult education for interreligious dialogue.

Clearly I envision such a model to be supportive of each individual's ongoing personal transformation, as well as to facilitate the commitment and skill for embracing various modalities of interreligious dialogue in the broader community. The model posits two group patterns in the process: the groups of people who come together to explore interreligious dialogue as well as the grouping that forms when the original group dialogues with others who are resources to this learning endeavor.

Crisis and concern both on the individual as well as the social levels provide fertile ground for growth and integration as well as a call for transformation, even if modest. Entering into a transformative process in a manner that embraces one's intellect, one's emotions, one's spirituality, and one's capabilities to act potentiates the investment in the learning process. As the encounter with commonalities and differences is essential to discovering common ground, it is imperative that these be integral to the dynamic from the very start. Adult learning is grounded in the premise that we are all subjects creating the path of our ongoing journey and thus a participative mode is essential.

Among the elements of the transformative model of adult education are: deepening relationships within a learning community, using various learning modes, connecting to core values, use of storytelling, some social analysis of the structures that impact the relationships between faith traditions, and embracing the choice toward transformation.

In the process of creating bonds and forming community one needs to unearth motivations for embarking on the journey, exploring assumptions, and enabling each individual to give voice to what he or she desires to articulate. The process must also include assessment of experiences offering support, challenge, and affirmation for moving into more constructive spaces, and the fostering of energy and openness for various learning modes.

Both the invitation to and the design of the learning experience need to embrace the engagement of the whole person: body, mind, and spirit. The ambience should create a space for attentive listening, allowing the individuals to find the words for offering their inner experience to themselves and others. The modes of learning should include: storytelling, input, personal reflection, personal sharing, group reflection and consensus-building, aesthetic offerings, symbols, cultural expressions, and exploration.

Consciously grounding the learning in core values is integral to taking steps in transformation and to discovering common ground as a community of learners and persons concerned for the social environment. Consciously touching on core values is integral to taking steps in transformation and to finding common ground. Attainment of common ground requires identifying the vision of what we hope for and what calls forth our commitment to both the attentiveness and generosity needed for transformation and the hard work of engaging in interreligious dialogue in the broader arenas of life.

Storytelling is a powerful modality for contextualizing the arena of mutual exploration and discovery as well as evoking a consciousness of meaning. It supports the recognition of paradoxes and conflicts that lie at the heart of our struggle to change. Storytelling is also a creative way of inviting others into mutual learning moments.

Becoming aware of some of the structural, historical, and cultural elements that underpin one's religious traditions and impact one's personal identities as a person of faith is vitally important. It is one of the elements that facilitates uncovering assumptions and perceptions and looking at them critically. With this, one paves the way for new conscious choices—thus the possibility of transformation. It is imperative that transformation be seen and embraced as integral to a life journey and consciously sought. Embracing conscious choice in transformation, sustaining mutuality in learning (*not* one dominant over the other) leads to the enhancing of the inner authority of the person. This can be the most significant outcome of the process.

The process needs to address the question of how the learning supports leadership in the community. Learning should foster deepened concern for our own issues, enabling us to see our own issues connected to the even wider circle of human concerns. We can then join with others in seeking creative resolutions to wider issues, utilizing group processes and skills for the service of others.

5

Planning for an Introduction to Encountering Other Faiths

Aims of This Process

The process of "Encountering Other Faiths" has as its under-pinning the stages of Deep-Dialogue (chapter 4), of "crossing over, entering the world of the other, experiencing the world of the other, then crossing back with an expanded vision, and attaining a radical paradigm shift." While this paradigm is a foundation, such depth of change cannot materialize within the short exposure and timeframe offered in this model for introducing interreligious dialogue. However, I do believe that the dynamic envisioned is solid and provides a form for the process. Thus the process prepares individuals for a crossing over and entering the world of the "other," offers an "audit" of previous simple experiences of crossing over and entering, provides an experience of shared space with the other, and finally guides the participants into a debriefing concerning that experience such that some integration and thus transformation may occur.

I believe that it is very important that Bennett's insights concerning the stages of entering into the world of the other inform the process design with a basic underlying sensitivity. It provides a framework for sensitivity to, understanding of, and response to reactions of defensiveness, and minimization. The process provides an invitation to and a model of acceptance of and adaptation to the "other," and also a forum in which to review experience. Some of the facets of Bennett's "helps to move to the next stage" are built into the design of this proposed model for entering into interreligious dialogue. Looking even briefly at Bennett's insights and findings also helps in understanding the costs of this journey of crossing over and back as well as of how one might build in personal and communal strength to carry this into the future.

The personal and spiritual development required for this faith journey is elucidated by Fowler's stages of faith development. By using his characterization of a person at stage three, this model encourages participants to understand where "they have come from" before the point of crossing over. It offers them insight about their motivations and desire to cross over, as well as about the need to attend to some of the stage three shadows as they step into the vulnerability of an unknown place. By utilizing insights from Fowler's work in this process for interreligious dialogue, I have attempted to empower participants to bear the psychic and spiritual costs of the crossing over, to deal with the threat that doing so poses to their familiar and comfortable existing worldviews, and to perceive and embrace the rewards of the deepened worldview they attain. By highlighting (all that is feasible within the scope of this process) stage five, I have attempted to enable participants to see that the journey is ongoing and offers yet more opportunities for the faithful journeyer. Finally, references to stage six support the cultivation of a vision of global ethics and solidarity and so provide a deeper appreciation for those giants of interreligious relations who have appeared from time to time, often in situations of major intercultural and/or interreligious tension, and, through the deep insight incarnated in their actions, have changed the course of world history.

Basic Assumptions

A desired outcome of this work on dialogue is deep compassion for the other, the other that begins with one's inner circle and extends beyond this to include the other in ever broader circles. Assumptions I have made concerning participation in this process of introduction to interreligious dialogue are as follows:

1. The process has been designed to be of benefit to members of a religious or faith tradition who, out of various motivations, have some interest in dialogue with others and for whom a general background in what interreligious dialogue is may be helpful.

2. I imagine the participants to be people who know about their own faith, at least at the high-school level or at the level of what would be required for the ritual of becoming a mature member of the faith community. The necessary educational level for dealing with the concepts presented is a high-school diploma.

3. I imagine participants to be currently in contact with their chosen faith or spiritual community and thus consider themselves involved in the living and learning experiences of their communities.

4. I imagine them to be people who have grown beyond Fowler's stage three of faith and have made some moves to interact with or on behalf of people who are in some ways different from themselves. Interest in interreligious dialogue evidences a faith level of Fowler's stage four.

5. I imagine them to be people who are likely to have commitments and priorities in their lives that demand their time and energy. At the same time, they are interested enough in effective interreligious encounter to prioritize time for this and have de-

cided to make a commitment to the work involved in the process.

6. I imagine that participants are likely to have a wide range of knowledge, from none or a little to quite a bit, of the following: the multireligious diversity in this nation, their city, or their local area; the basic tenets, practices, and worldviews of other faiths; current perspectives of their own faith; and the nature and the practices of interreligious dialogue. The format of this process can encompass this range of knowledge.

I want to acknowledge a bias that I hold. My bias is that religion is sufficiently culturally connected that one needs to tailor any pedagogical material and process in "Encountering Other Faiths" to each unique religious grouping.

Basic Principles

1. The journey into interreligious dialogue has to be well-grounded in the faith journey of the individual, the call to love as inspired by the faith tradition, and the vision of humans as brothers and sisters to each other. Motivational forces might include: the exploration of human goodness as it searches for the transcendent and a better world, the desire to know more about other faiths, and the desire to do what one can to counteract negative effects of religious fundamentalism and oppression. For some people, the motivation may stem from relationship with a significant other who has become or is an adherent of a different faith from their own.

2. The journey toward being a person of interreligious dialogue will occur best, like other such transformations, in the ambiance of

a group. Here one experiences: affirmation, critique, bonding, energy, example, acceptance, encouragement in making necessary changes, witness and celebration, and a forum where insights multiply. Thus the process is oriented to group forums, not individual forums.

3. The nature of the journey needs to be articulated. One might assume that some people want to become fully functional in stage four of Fowler's stages of faith and some hope to be able to exercise the abilities of a stage-five person. Thus the process should, in the end, support the challenge to interact with others at the level of stage five.

4. Participants are expected to have in-depth knowledge of their own faith and some knowledge of at least one other faith tradition. In addition, they should have the ability to listen to the other with empathy and openness and be able to speak of their own faith in language comprehensible to the other. Finally, they should be acquainted with the three/four modalities of dialogue and have the ability to engage in some of them.

5. The sessions should address the attitudes and implement the skills of the good dialogue.

6. For maximum benefit from the learning situation, there needs to be congruence between the major themes highlighted for study of the different religions and the interests of the participants.

7. The design of the process needs to facilitate the participants' goal of becoming persons who can engage interreligious dialogue that embraces the modalities of: neighborliness, collaboration in light of a common cause, shared spiritual and aesthetic experiences, and a beginning understanding of the commonalities and differences in belief systems.

8. Somewhere in the process, the issues of unawareness of the realities of other religious traditions, defensiveness in encounters with those of other religions, prejudices, generalizations that we are really all alike, and the tendency to be absolutist oneself need to be woven in through the various steps of the process. I do believe that this is not difficult to do.

9. For maximum benefit, the participants' experience of this process should be shared in an ongoing way with the wider faith community for support, for witness, for mutual engagement where possible.

10. The facilitation of the process is supported when two persons share this role. The facilitators undertake to prepare, to name and delegate tasks, to highlight readings, and to oversee the general flow of the sessions for the benefit of the participants.

A good educational process for cultivating interreligious dialogue at the grassroots level will involve individuals working in groups. One of the observations made in relation to movement from a faith stance enmeshed in one's faith community to one where an individual takes initiative and responsibility engendered by a deeper inner authority is that this move is often stymied by the aloneness and loneliness of such a position. In these postmodern times, some faith communities are beginning not only to tolerate such personal development but are supporting it. Doing this type of study in groups offsets some of the "belonging" type losses as one leaves stage three. It also supports nuclei of stage-four communities and may engender some stage-five talents for the benefit of the wider community.

Therefore the application of group process principles is important here. Insights from other disciplines also need to be woven in, particularly insights with regard to faith development and the conversion process and intercultural competencies applied not only to culture but to religion as well. These major threads need to be harmonized in the endeavor. The endeavor itself can flounder or be fractured unless there is clear grounding. I suggest that each faith tradition establish and nurture such grounding throughout the process.

Applications

The model that follows in chapter 6 is designed to be consistent with the assumptions and principles offered above. In order to determine its effectiveness and in order to refine it further, the piloting of this model is being assessed in light of results, methods, style, content, and overall process. These assessments will further shape the process to ensure its relevance to the needs of people today.

I foresee that engagement with this model would be of interest to a range of people within faith communities, such as:

- Local faith communities with animation or affirmation by the community's leadership
- Local ecumenical study groups as they plan future content for their agenda
- Those having responsibilities or holding mandates for the coordination or animation of interreligious dialogue among adherents of their own faith and/or in concert with the efforts of their counterparts of other faith traditions
- Teachers or other professionals who are drawn to undertake the ministry of interreligious dialogue

The talents and skills important in piloting and further shaping an introduction to interreligious dialogue such as this include a certain maturity of faith and a college level of education or the equivalent in self-education and experience in interacting with those of other faith traditions. Also important are availability and a willingness to plan and prepare for sessions with the groups. Some orientation to the model, such as attendance at a workshop or conversations with people familiar with the model, would surely enhance the ease and effectiveness of its implementation.

The model as presented in chapter 6 and the assumptions that underlie it should be reviewed prior to beginning the process with each unique group.

6
Encountering Other Faiths

The model presented in this chapter has been designed for communities desiring to begin an exploration of interreligious engagement. The process, which in this presentation and format is divided into nine sessions, may vary in accord with circumstances. It is essential, however, to allow for a minimum of two hours for each session as well as the time needed to prepare for engaging in the sessions.

The model lends itself to adjustments in accord with an assessment of each group's skills and needs. Examples of adjustments could include:

- Deleting a step within a session if the group has already achieved the goal of that step
- Dividing the content of a particular session into two or more sessions to accommodate the availability of the participants
- Altering the sequence of the sessions in response to the flow of developments, interests, and needs within the group
- Adding activities, such as individually undertaken interreligious engagements between sessions with debriefing in the group setting

- Deleting a session (although it is important to ensure that the learning inherent in that session can be obtained in alternative ways)

The process itself has a built-in evaluation that will provide information to guide the further reshaping of the process.

SESSION ONE
Gathering in Faith

Purpose

Welcome, exploration of hopes and expectations and planning for the seminar

Participant Objectives

- To welcome one another and share expectations
- To set goals for the program
- To establish basic parameters for meetings
- To plan for gathering information about religious diversity in their areas of interest

Background and Resource Materials for Session One

- Reading: "The Meaning of Interreligious Dialogue," chapter 2
- Reading: "Basic Assumptions" and "Basic Principles" of "Encountering Other Faiths," chapter 5

PROCESS

Welcome by sponsors and facilitators
- Welcome
- Introduction, history of coming together and of undertaking this process
- Introductions—all participating, with facilitators modeling process
    - Please give your name, tell where you grew up, and something about your neighborhood.

– Share with the group an early encounter with a person of a different faith or religion.

Exploring motivations and expectations

- In the large group, explore questions: What draws me or brings me to this process? What expectations do I have for this process?
- Observe the patterns in the expectations. Prioritize the expectations.
- Using the prioritized expectations, develop three to four achievable goals for the group's process.

The meaning of interreligious dialogue

- The facilitator presents highlights of the reading, "The Meaning of Interreligious Dialogue."
- The facilitator reviews assumptions, principles, and roles inherent to the seminar process.

Establish parameters for the process

- Dates, times and location of sessions
- Format of sessions
- Naming various responsibilities: for ambiance, gathering ritual, refreshments

Establish process for gaining information concerning religious diversity in the area of group interest, neighborhood, county, interreligious coalition, or other

- Name the area.
- Identify the information the group already has.
- Determine what additional information is needed and how participants will cooperate in obtaining this. Two helpful ways to do this are: participant observations as they travel within the area of concern and the Internet site: <http://www.worshiphere.org>.

- Ask two people to collate the information and format it for Session Three.

Homework for Session Two

- Review of personal interreligious encounter—simple write-up of encounter with a person of another faith
- Reading: "The United States and the Relevance and Imperative of Interreligious Dialogue," chapter 1
- Begin the gathering of data regarding religious diversity in the area of concern.

SESSION TWO
Assessing Our Encounters with People of Other Faiths

Purpose

To develop insights about interreligious encounters and to become acquainted with sources of information about the beliefs, practices, and structure of other faith traditions

Participant Objectives

- To share accounts of personal encounters with those of other faith traditions and to learn from these encounters
- To become acquainted with guidelines for interfaith dialogue
- To become acquainted with informative, concise resources on major religious traditions

Background and Resource Material for Session Two

- Simple write-up (by each participant) of encounter with a person of another faith
- Reading: "The United States and the Relevance and Imperative of Interreligious Dialogue," chapter 1
- "Ground Rules of Interreligious Dialogue," chapter 2
- References for concise materials on major faith traditions, gathered by facilitator

PROCESS

Review of expectations and goals generated in Session One

Facilitator presents highlights of "The United States and the Relevance and Imperative of Interreligious Dialogue"

Process of exploring personal interreligious encounters
- In small groups, each participant presents a copy of his or her encounter with a person of another faith; time is given for reading.
- Presenter highlights the encounter; listeners ask questions for clarification; presenter offers clarifications.
- Listeners offer insights; presenter responds.
- The above process is repeated with each presenter.
- The group takes note of shared insights about dialogue with others.

In large group, members share insights and what they have learned
- Members are invited to share insights and what they have learned.
- Large group considers: What attitudes and behaviors lead to a positive outcome from interreligious encounters? What attitudes and behaviors are detrimental to a positive outcome from interreligious encounters?

Facilitator introduces the "Ground Rules of Interreligious Dialogue"
- After input, buzz sessions take place in large group.
- Participants explore implications and offer insights about applications in real life situations.

Homework for Session Three

- Preparation of data concerning diversity of worshiping communities in area of interest and concern
- Reading: "Modalities of Interreligious Dialogue," chapter 2

SESSION THREE
Exploring Religious Diversity within Our Locale

Purpose

To become acquainted with the presence of other faith traditions within our area of interest and to become aware of the implications of this presence in light of the modalities of interreligious dialogue

Participant Objectives

- To review and learn from the data concerning the presence of people of other faith traditions within the area of interest
- To grow in awareness of the implications and potential contained in this data
- To become acquainted with themes that lend themselves to exchange between those of different religious traditions

Background and Resource Material for Session Three

- Data regarding religious diversity in area of group interest
- "The United States and Religious Diversity," from chapter 1
- Reading: "Modalities of Interreligious Dialogue," chapter 2
- Reading: "Major Themes of Exploration," chapter 2

PROCESS

Review and exploration of the data concerning the presence of various faith traditions within the area of interest
- Those who have collated the material present their summary to the group.
- Participants offer insights as to the adequacy of the data, implications of the data, and applications of information obtained.

Facilitator presents highlights of the "Modalities of Interreligious Dialogue"

- In small groups participants focus on the different modalities of interreligious dialogue, members consider their own experiences with these modalities and what potential there is for furthering each modality within the area of interest or concern.
- Small groups summarize their insights. These insights are shared with the large group.

Major Themes of Exploration for Use in Interreligious Dialogue

- Simple introduction by facilitator
- Consideration of what themes will be used for exploration in Session Four

Homework for Session Four

- Review reading: "Major Themes of Exploration," chapter 2
- Refresh acquaintance with "Ground Rules of Interreligious Dialogue"

SESSION FOUR
Treasuring Our Faith Heritage

Purpose

To articulate and affirm the authenticity and relevance of aspects of one's own faith; to cultivate confidence, openness, and interest in the work of getting to know persons of other faith traditions

Participant Objectives

- To become acquainted with the major themes to be used in exploring one's own and others' faith traditions
- To study one of the themes as members of a unique faith tradition
- To dialogue about one or more of the themes

Background and Resource Material for Session Four

- Reading: "Major Themes of Exploration," chapter 2
- Concise information on faith traditions presented by individuals invited to dialogue in Session Five

PROCESS

Selecting theme for exploration within the group
- Participants select (a) theme(s) for exploration.
- Facilitator reminds the participants of "Ground Rules of Interreligious Dialogue."

Exploration of theme in small groups of three or more persons

- Facilitator offers simple, clear guidelines for discussion
  - Questions: How does one engage this theme personally? How does my identity as a person of faith support my engagement in this theme?
  - Facilitator highlights the questions given with the selected theme.
  - Large group shares insights on what participants have learned, particularly with regard to commonalities and differences discovered.

Presenter introduces the idea of search for common ground

- Group selects themes for dialogue with guests in Session Five.

Homework for Session Five

- Read concise background material on religious traditions of those invited
- Participants take responsibility to become personally acquainted with the persons invited and acquaint the guests with the focus theme of the dialogue.

SESSION FIVE
Engaging in Dialogue with People of Another Faith

Purpose

To enter into a dialogue of faith and to open oneself to the truth, beauty, and goodness in different religious traditions; to begin to appreciate both shared commonalities and differences

Participant Objectives

- To meet with persons of other faith traditions and begin dialogic conversations with them
- To gain a foundation for further possible exchanges and engagement among those present

Background and Resources for Session Five

- Information on religious traditions of invited guests
- "Ground Rules of Interreligious Dialogue," chapter 2

PROCESS

Welcome and introductions
- Welcome and introduction of guests
- Self-introductions of each guest and participant
- Participants give their names, religious or spiritual affiliations (if several are present), and share what makes them interested in interreligious dialogue

In small, mixed groups (alternatively, the full large group and a panel of guests)
- Guests and groups members present their views on the theme chosen for dialogue.

- Questions for clarification are entertained. These are preceded by mirroring back to the speaker what he or she has said and obtaining the speaker's verification of the questioner's understanding of what was conveyed.
- Free flowing discussion by all is invited.
- Small groups consider: highlights of their discussion, what they share in common, where participant expressions were different from one another.

Small group findings are shared in the large group
- What discoveries have participants made with respect to the commonalities and differences shared among them on this theme?
- What insights do they have with regard to finding common ground?

Consideration of possibilities for further encounters and further collaboration between those of different faith traditions
- In large group, brainstorming of avenues of further encounters with, interaction between members of the different faith communities
- Test for viability of the different alternatives

Expression of gratitude to the guests for their presence and contributions

Homework for Session Six

- Participants reflect on the sharing that took place in Session Five: What commonalities were discovered? What differences were discovered? What is the nature of those differences?
- Ideas concerning further collaboration with others are noted and printed up for use in Session Six.

SESSION SIX
Exploring Common Ground with People of Other Faiths

Purpose

To confirm the discovery of common ground and the nature of the dialogue that fosters common ground; to articulate patterns of constructive dialogue and collaborative action with members of other religious traditions

Participant Objectives

- To integrate the learning from Session Five
- To envision ways of further collaboration within the area of interest and concern

Background and Resource Materials for Session Six

- Participant reflections on dialogue in Session Five
- Reading: "Introduction to Common Ground," chapter 2
- Collation of ideas for further collaboration within the group's areas of interest and concern

PROCESS

Facilitator presents highlights of "Introduction to Common Ground"

Debriefing experiences of dialogue with those of other faiths
- In small groups, participants share their experience of dialogue in Session Five
  - Feelings experienced, understanding gained
  - Commonalities discovered; differences discovered; the nature of the differences

- Learning in relation to common ground
- Hopes and expectations regarding further engagement
  with faith groups in the area

In large group, members collate what they have learned in small groups

- Listen to reports from the small group, note similarities and complementarities.
- Generate the group's own wisdom about working toward common ground.

Envisioning a future with others

- In the large group, consider future collaboration with those of other faiths: What are the practical elements of the vision we see for the future? What are the hindrances to this practical vision? What directions would be helpful in moving toward the future?

Homework for Session Seven

- Reading: "Fowler's Stages of Faith and Interreligious Dialogue," summarized from chapter 4
- Personal reflection:
  - Since the time of high school, what significant deepening of faith have I experienced? How has this experience transformed me? What experiences and persons helped in that transformation?
  - How has participation in the process of "Encountering Other Faiths" influenced my own faith?
  - How has "Encountering Other Faiths" impacted my beliefs and attitudes toward people of other religious traditions? How has it influenced my ongoing commitment to the future?

SESSION SEVEN
Learning from Our Experiences of Deepening Faith

Purpose

To explore the ground for commitment to interreligious engagement and/or dialogue as an experience of deeper faith; to plan for interfacing this commitment with the mission of my larger community

Participant Objectives

- To explore personal faith experiences, and to discern whether these are deepening through interreligious engagement
- To assess the attainment of group goals thus far

Background and Resource Material for Session Seven

- Reflections concerning personal experiences in deepening faith in general and in relation to "Encountering Other Faiths"
- "Fowler's Stages of Faith and Interreligious Dialogue," summarized from chapter 4

PROCESS

Exploring personal growth in faith
- In groups of three or more, share an experience of growth in faith, since the time of high school: What was the transformation you experienced? What experiences, persons helped in that transformation?

- Deepening faith and "Encountering Other Faiths"
  - During the seven sessions experienced thus far, what one or two experiences have been significant for you or have impacted you strongly?
  - In what ways have these experiences affected your own faith?
- Small groups share in large group what they have learned

Assessing "Encountering Other Faiths" in light of its impact on dialogue with others

- Sharing in small groups:
  - In what ways has the experience of "Encountering Other Faiths" had an impact on your beliefs and attitudes toward people of other religious traditions?
  - In what ways has your faith been deepened through the process? What has been helpful? What could be more helpful?

Sharing the experience of "Encountering Other Faiths"

- In the large group, consider how to share with the wider faith community aspects of this experience and what has been learned: Who? What? When? How?

Assessing goals

- In the large group, review and assess how goals set in Session One have been addressed.

Homework for Session Eight

- Evaluation of the design and process of "Encountering Other Faiths":
  - Reviewing the program in general: How has it fostered your understanding of interreligious dialogue?

- What have been the three main emphases of the program for you? For each of these consider the questions: In what ways has each of these proved helpful? In what ways has it been *un*helpful?
- Considering the overall design: Has it been clear? Has it been user-friendly?
- What attitudes and skills have you acquired as a result of participating in the program?
• Reading: "Stages of Interreligious Dialogue," chapter 4

SESSION EIGHT
Responding to Our "Call" to Interreligious Dialogue

Purpose

To gain an overall picture of the process of "Encountering Other Faiths"; to critique the process; to see how the process can be used to help others in becoming acquainted with interreligious dialogue

Participant Objectives

- To identify the design and processes used in this seminar
- To articulate and confirm the most usable of these processes and to identify a process that might best support participants in facilitating others' interest and participation
- To identify resources for persons desiring to develop skills in facilitating interreligious dialogue

Background and Resource Material for Session Eight

- Personal evaluation of the process of "Encountering Other Faiths"
- Reading: "Stages of Interreligious Dialogue," chapter 4

PROCESS

Assessment of the process for "Encountering Other Faiths"
- Using participants' personal reflections, small groups share their personal responses in assessing the process:
  - How has the program fostered interreligious dialogue?
  - What has been helpful, unhelpful?

- Overall, has the process been clear and user-friendly? In what ways?
- What attitudes and skills have participants acquired?
- Sharing of observations with respect to what participants have learned
- Small groups develop recommendations for a process for supporting persons who are interested in beginning interreligious dialogue.
- Small groups share their findings and recommendations with the large group.
- The large group considers: What would make this a more usable process? How can participants use these recommendations as tools for their own work?

Stages of interreligious dialogue
- The stages of interreligious dialogue (see chapter 4) are highlighted by the facilitator.
- In buzz groups, participants reflect on how their experience contributes to understanding these stages of interreligious dialogue.
- Findings are shared with the large group.

Homework for Session Nine
- Review of Miriam Therese Winter's "Witnessing to the Spirit: Reflections on an Emerging American Spirituality," from *11 September—Religious Perspectives on the Causes and Consequences*, highlighted in chapter 1, or the *Earth Charter*, a United Nations document created by the largest consultation ever achieved across the globe. It articulates best principles and practices for creating a global society that is sustainable and peaceful. <http://www.earthcharter.org>.

- Each person agrees to become acquainted with one expression of each of the tenets of: universal love, compassion, justice, and charity of his or her own faith tradition and of another faith tradition. Each of these is written on a $5\frac{1}{2}$" x 8" piece of paper, with one tenet on each sheet of paper.
- Each person meets with a person of another religious tradition and considers the question: What four principles do you both agree would form the basis of an approach to life issues that would foster greater access to justice for all? These four principles are noted on $5\frac{1}{2}$" x 8" sheets of paper, one to each sheet.

SESSION NINE
Envisioning a New World Reality—
Deepening Kinship, Collaborating for the Common Good

Purpose

To confirm tenets of universal love, compassion, justice, and charity within faith traditions and the potential for collaboration across interfaith boundaries for the common good

Participant Objectives

- To become acquainted with the common good that can come alive through the collaborative work of women and men of different religious and/or ideological traditions
- To begin to grasp the blessings, opportunities, and challenges for the American people posed by the pluriformity of America's religious traditions

Background and Resource Material for Session Nine

- Participants' work on tenets from at least two different religious traditions
- Participants' work on an approach to life developed in dialogue with someone of another faith tradition
- Readings: highlights of Miriam Therese Winter's "Witnessing to the Spirit: Reflections on an Emerging American Spirituality," from *11 September—Religious Perspectives on the Causes and Consequences* from chapter 1 and the *Earth Charter*

PROCESS

Tenets of faith traditions
- In the large group, participants share their work on the tenets of universal love, compassion, justice, and charity, grouping

the 5$^1/_2$" x 8" sheets of paper on newsprint under the same headings. These are later typed up and given to participants.

Considering the blessings and challenges of interreligious engagement

- Participants share in the large group their principles for a more just society, noted on the 5$^1/_2$" x 8" sheets of paper.
- Themes are identified and contributions grouped in accord with themes. All papers relating to the same theme are attached to one piece of newsprint.
- Small groups work on a theme, harmonizing the different contributions and reaching a consensus on an articulation that honors the various contributions.
- The work of the small groups is collated in the large group. Discussion on the implications of this work follows.

Review of readings

- Participants form small groups, joining with those who have worked on the same document.
- Group members share their insights. These are collated and five insights are selected and noted on newsprint in order to share them with the large group.
- In the large group, what has been learned in the small groups is shared. The participants consider: What promise does such work hold for us in the twenty-first century? What are some of the difficulties in implementing these approaches?

Ritual of Commitment

Closing

Concluding Thoughts

By the close of the ninth session, one should be confident that participants:

- Have been sensitized to the reality of truth, beauty, and goodness that is inherent in another faith or other faiths
- Are more disposed to empathy with and appreciation of persons of other faiths and more effectively disposed to collaborating with them
- Understand the various modalities of interreligious dialogue and are able to both assess their present level of engagement and think creatively about still other avenues of engagement
- Have been exposed to some of the foundational beliefs and attitudes that could suggest a non-absolutist stance in relation to other religious traditions
- Have a sense of the challenge and responsibility that they and adherents of other religious traditions face with respect to fostering a more viable future for the local, national, and global community
- Have become acquainted or made friends with one or more persons of another religious tradition and thus have created a small building block toward a multifaith community
- Have experienced a deepening of their own faith and its articulation

7

A New Beginning

At this point in the book, you, the reader, may be expecting a conclusion, an ending. But no, this is only a beginning. Humanity is beginning again a new phase of its journey arising out of new consciousnesses and new yearnings. In fact, there are already all kinds of as yet random forays into this future. These are insightful, heartfelt, and purposeful. They are small and not so small movements across and through the boundaries of religious exclusivism. They are coalescing into a rainbow of promise, creativity, beauty, and peace. This rainbow is a sign in the heavens and in our hearts that we are blessed, that we are accompanied in the brave and sometimes faltering steps we take on this journey.

In the process of developing this model for introducing interested men and women to the wonderful world of interreligious dialogue, I have become acutely aware of how important such a process can be to the moral and spiritual development of people of faith today. Grassroots participation in interreligious dialogue can be of immense benefit to human life in the twenty-first century. But any model for introducing people to interreligious dialogue has to be both authentic and relevant.

A realistic decision to undertake such an endeavor depends initially on the availability of a model for implementation and second on marketing and piloting the model. Third, the model needs to be continually reshaped as insights from experience dictate.

Chapter 6 of this book serves as a basis for a participant's manual for adult learning sessions. The model incorporates relevant texts from earlier chapters. To emphasize the fourfold nature of interreligious dialogue, I have entitled the model "Encountering Other Faiths."

A program that supports the actual initiation of interfaith dialogue groups can well follow the process outlined in "Encountering Other Faiths." A similar process, the Philadelphia Model of Interfaith Dialogue, has been in use among Catholics and Jews in the Philadelphia area for many years. With the institution of the Interfaith Center of Greater Philadelphia, the original process of the Interfaith Lay Dialogue Project has now been broadened to include more faith traditions.

Participation in interfaith dialogue groups can lead to further steps, including the development of the skills of facilitation and the undertaking of a commitment to encourage the development of new ventures in interreligious dialogue in other areas.

I trust that with worldwide awareness of the need to reach out to others beyond our own faith traditions these projects will be found to be a small building block toward a new world community.

> In this community I envision brothers and sisters looking
> into each other's eyes.

> A look that promises a welcoming place to gather,
> to be at home, to unite, to center into a passion for
> justice, to grieve and to rejoice, to create a common
> spirituality, and to protect the sacred spaces of its
> multiple faith heritages.

> A look that affirms one another's right to be
> Unique, cooperative, dissenting, dialoguing
> Coalescing around a new vision and common ground.

A look that challenges each
to claim his or her own history and to listen to the
    unfolding story,
to move from apathy to engaged creativity, from
    cynicism to prudent optimism,
from despair to hope, from injustice to justice,
from hate to forgiveness and love, from chaos to
    dynamic harmony.

I envision a long journey, people taking steps,
voting Yes with their feet, and their heads and hands and
    hearts,
persons engaged with one another across cherished
    uniqueness,
engendering a vibrant spirit, a spirit that outstrips all
    meaning we have yet known.

This is the call of interreligious engagement.

Notes

Chapter One

1. John L. Allen, Jr., "Pluralism Conference Report," *National Catholic Reporter* (September 12, 2003).

2. Ibid.

3. Ibid.

4. Ibid.

5. Ibid.

6. Ibid.

7. Religions for Peace, "The Kyoto Declaration on Confronting Violence and Advancing Shared Security," <http://www.wcrp.org/about/assemblies/kyoto-2006>, 2–4.

8. Ibid., 5.

9. Center for the Study of Religious Life, *Dialogue on Mission* (Chicago: Claretian Publications, 2000), 17–18.

10. John Borelli, "The Catholic Church and Interreligious Relations" Presentation, Summer Studies, Christ the King Seminary, Buffalo, NY, July 8, 2003, 3.

11. I was present at the 2005 International Scholars Meeting on the Holocaust (Philadelphia, March 2005).

12. Google results for "Muslims against September 11 attacks" net 2,110,000 entries. The Council on American-Islamic Relations has documented many Muslim condemnations of the September 11th attacks. This documentation can be found at <http://www.cair-net.org/html/911statements.html>.

13. Institute for Jewish and Community Research, "Growth and Vitality of Jewish Peoplehood," <http://www.jewishresearch.org/projects_growth.htm>, 3–7.

14. Center for the Study of Religious Life, *Dialogue on Mission* (Chicago: Claretian Publications, 2000), 39.

Chapter Two

1. Leonard Swidler and Paul Mojzes, *The Study of Religion in an Age of Global Dialogue* (Philadelphia: Temple University Press, 2000), 174–77.

2. Pontifical Council for Inter-religious Dialogue, "Dialogue and Proclamation," <http://www.vatican.va/roman_curia/pontifical_councils/interelg/documents/rc_pc_interelg_doc_19051991_dialogue-and-proclamation_en.html>, no. 42.

3. Swidler and Mojzes, *The Study of Religion*, 156–59.

4. Ibid., 158.

5. Ibid., 160.

6. Ibid., 161.

Chapter Three

1. Nadira K.Charaniya and Jane West Walsh, "Adult Learning in the Context of the Interreligious Dialogue Process: A Collaborative Research Study Involving Christians, Jews and Muslims," 2001 AERC Proceedings, <http://www.edst.educ.ubc.ca/aerc/2001/2001charaniya.htm>, 1.

2. Ibid., 2.

3. Ibid., 3.

4. Ibid., 6.

5. Medical Mission Sisters, *Core Aspects of MMS Spirituality* (Philadelphia: Medical Mission Sisters, 2001), 96–97.

Chapter Four

1. Milton Bennett, "Towards Ethnorelativism: A Developmental Model of Intercultural Sensitivity," in *Education for the Intercultural Experience*, ed. Michael R. Paige (Yarmouth, ME: Intercultural Press, 1993), 10.

2. Ibid., 26.

3. Ibid., 22.

4. Ibid., 30.

5. Merriam-Webster, *Webster's Ninth New Collegiate Dictionary* (Springfield, MA: Merriam-Webster Inc., 1984), 906.

6. Bennett, M., "Towards Ethnorelativism," 35.

7. Janet Bennett, "Cultural Marginality: Identity Issues in Intercultural Training," in *Education for Intercultural Experience*, ed. Michael R. Paige (Yarmouth, ME: Intercultural Press, 1993), 117.

8. Ibid., 116.

9. Ibid., 111.

10. Fowler's landmark research in the process of faith development led to the articulation of a six-stage paradigm. This is well documented in his book, *Stages of Faith*. Fowler's stages have become common parlance for all those in the field, such that the mention of the number of the stage evokes an immediate recall of the content of that stage. In his book, *Becoming Adult, Becoming Christian*, published in 2000, Fowler has revised these stages such that stage one is divided into two stages: Primal faith and Intuitive-Projective faith. Since this new category of stages is not yet easily recognizable, this book will use Fowler's original delineation of stages.

11. James Fowler, *Stages of Faith* (San Francisco: HarperSanFrancisco, 1981), 92.

12. Ibid., 200.

13. Ibid., 183.

14. Ibid., 198.

15. Ibid.

16. Ibid., 200.

17. Leonard Swidler and Paul Mojzes, *The Study of Religion in an Age of Global Dialogue* (Philadelphia: Temple University Press, 2000), 41.

18. Ibid., 147.

19. Ibid., 163–66.

20. Fowler, *Stages of Faith*, 200.

21. Bennett, J. "Cultural Marginality," 116.

22. Dorothy Ettling, "Leadership for Action: Wedding Adult Education and Social Change," 2001 AERC Proceedings, <http://www.edst.educ.ubc.ca/aerc/2001/2001ettling.htm>, 1.

Bibliography

Alfred, Mary V. "Epistemology, Learning, and Self-Development among Immigrant Women of Color: The Case of the British Caribbean Women in the United States." 2001 AERC Proceedings, <http://www.edst. educ.ubc.ca/aerc/2001/2001 alfred.htm>.

Allen, John L., Jr. "Pluralism Conference Report." *National Catholic Reporter.* September 12, 2003.

Armstrong, Joseph L. "Collaborative Learning from the Participants' Perspective." 2001 AERC Proceedings, <http://www.edst.educ.ubc.ca/aerc/2001/2001armstrong.htm>.

Barnes, Michael, SJ. *Theology and the Dialogue of Religions.* Cambridge: Cambridge University Press, 2002.

———. *Walking in the City.* New Delhi: Cambridge Press, 1999.

Bennett, Janet M. "Cultural Marginality: Identity Issues in Intercultural Training." In *Education for the Intercultural Experience,* ed. Michael R. Paige. Yarmouth, ME: Intercultural Press, 1993.

Bennett, Milton. "Towards Ethnorelativism: A Developmental Model of Intercultural Sensitivity. In *Education for the Intercultural Experience,* ed. Michael R. Paige. Yarmouth, ME: Intercultural Press, 1993.

Borelli, John. "The Catholic Church and Interreligious Relations." Presentation, Summer Studies, Christ the King Seminary, East Aurora, NY, July 8, 2003.

————, ed. *Handbook for Interreligious Dialogue*. Morristown, NJ: Silver Burdett & Ginn, 1988.

Bristow, Edward, ed. *No Religion Is an Island*. New York: Fordham University Press, 1998.

Brooks, Annie, and Carolyn Clark. "Narrative Dimensions of Transformative Learning." 2001 AERC Proceedings, <http://www.edst.educ.ubc.ca/aerc/2001/2001brooks.htm>.

Center for the Study of Religious Life. *Dialogue on Mission*. Chicago: Claretian Publications, 2000.

Charaniya, Nadira K., and Jane West Walsh. "Adult Learning in the Context of the Interreligious Dialogue Process: A Collaborative Research Study Involving Christians, Jews and Muslims." 2001 AERC Proceedings, <http://www.edst.educ.ubc.ca/aerc/2001/2001charaniya.htm>.

Ettling, Dorothy. "Leadership for Action: Wedding Adult Education and Social Change." 2001 AERC Proceedings, <http://www.edst.educ.ubc.ca/aerc/2001/2001ettling.htm>.

"A Familiar Concern!" *The American Muslim* 2/5 (December 2001), <http://www.americanmuslim.org/9editorial9.html>.

Fowler, James. *Becoming Adult, Becoming Christian*. San Francisco: Jossey-Bass, 2000.

————. *Stages of Faith*. San Francisco: HarperSanFrancisco, 1981.

"The Growth and Vitality of Jewish Peoplehood." Institute for Jewish and Community Research, 2006, <http://www.jewishresearch.org/projects_growth.htm>.

Hellwig, Monika. *Understanding Catholicism*. Mahwah, NJ: Paulist Press, 2002.

Hick, John. *Philosophy of Religion*. New Delhi: Prentice-Hall, 1981.

Interfaith Dialogue—A Manual for Facilitators and Sponsors. Philadelphia: Interfaith Lay Dialogue Project, 2004.

"The Kyoto Declaration on Confronting Violence and Advancing Shared Security." Religions for Peace Eighth World Assembly, 2006, <http://www.wcrp.org/about/assemblies/kyoto-2006>.

Markham, Ian S. *A Theology of Engagement.* Oxford: Blackwell Publishing, 2003.

Markham, Ian, and Ibrahim M. Abu-Rabi', eds. *11 September— Religious Perspectives on the Causes and Consequences.* Oxford: Oneworld Publications, 2002.

Medical Mission Sisters. *Core Aspects of MMS Spirituality.* Philadelphia: Medical Mission Sisters, 2001.

Mojzes, Paul. "The What and How of Dialogue." In *Interreligious Dialogue*, ed. M. Darrol Bryant and Frank Flinn. New York: Paragon House, 1989.

"Muslim World Condemns Attacks on U.S." *IslamOnline*, <http://www.islamonline.net/English/News/2001-09/13/article18.shtml>.

Paige, Michael R., ed. *Education for the Intercultural Experience.* Yarmouth, ME: Intercultural Press, 1993.

Pontifical Council for Inter-religious Dialogue. "Dialogue and Proclamation," 1991, <http://www.vatican.va/roman_curia/pontifical_councils/interelg/documents/rc_pc_interelg_doc_19051991_dialogue-and-proclamation_en.html>.

Swidler, Leonard. *After the Absolute.* Minneapolis: Fortress Press, 1990.

―――, ed. *For All Life—Toward a Universal Declaration of a Global Ethic.* Ashland, OR: White Cloud Press, 1999.

―――, ed. *Toward a Universal Theology of Religion.* Maryknoll, NY: Orbis Books, 1987.

Swidler, Leonard, and Ashok Gangadean. *The Technology of Deep-Dialogue/Critical Thinking.* Philadelphia: Global Dialogue Institute, 2000.

Swidler, Leonard, and Paul Mojzes. *The Study of Religion in An Age of Global Dialogue*. Philadelphia: Temple University Press, 2000.

Taylor, Edward W., John Dirkx, and Daniel Pratt. "Personal Pedagogical Systems: Core Beliefs, Foundational Knowledge, and Informal Theories of Teaching." 2001 AERC Proceedings, <http://www.edst.educ.ubc.ca/aerc/2001/2001taylor.htm>.

Tempesta, Martha Strittmatter. "A Phenomenological Study of Learning Experiences of Leaders within a Social Movement." 2001 AERC Proceedings, <http://www.edst.educ.ubc.ca/aerc/2001/2001tempesta.htm>.

Tisdell, Elizabeth J., Derise Tolliver, and Silvia Villa. "Toward a Culturally Relevant and Spiritually Grounded Theory of Teaching for Social Transformation and Transformational Learning." 2001 AERC Proceedings, <http://www.edst.educ.ubc.ca/aerc/2001/2001tisdell.htm>.

Walsh, John. *Evangelization and Justice*. Maryknoll, NY: Orbis Books, 1982.

Webster's Ninth New Collegiate Dictionary. Springfield, MA: Merriam-Webster Inc., 1984.

Winter, Miriam Therese. "Witnessing to the Spirit: Reflections on an Emerging American Spirituality." In *11 September — Religious Perspectives on the Causes and Consequences*, ed. Ian Markham and Ibrahim M. Abu-Rabi´. Oxford: Oneworld Publications, 2002.

Ziegahn, Linda. "Reflection and Transformation in the Intercultural Context." 2001 AERC Proceedings, <http://www.edst.educ.ubc.ca/aerc/2001/2001ziegahn.htm>.